Be careful what's coming

out of your mouth with

No **"IF"** or **"But"**

BY

Normand Dallaire

BOOKS ACADEMY
LEARNING LIFE FROM EVERY PAGE

BOOKS ACADEMY
LEARNING LIFE FROM EVERY PAGE

Copyright © 2025 by Normand Dallaire

Books Academy LLC

112 SW HK Dodgen Loop, Temple, Texas 76504

Hotline: (254) 800-1189

Ordering Information: Quantity sales. Special discounts are available on quantity purchases by corporations, associations, and others. For details, contact the publisher at the address above.

Printed in the United States of America.

ISBN: Softcover: 978-1-968807-24-5

                    eBook: 978-1-968807-25-2

Library of Congress Control Number: 2025919676

TABLE OF CONTENTS

DEDICATION

I dedicate this book to those who like to argue. I will give you a chance to go ahead and do it. I can take it, as long as nobody lies to try to win the conversation point. Also, when you will argue with an honest heart, I'll do the same, FAIR IS FAIR.

Normand.

PREFACE

This is another part of that series of books; with no "IF" or "BUT" series, and it is for you to added more knowledge on top of that you already have from the same subject. There is quite some important information for you to know. Some of these subjects will be touching subjects, and for some other sensitive subjects. I am coming after the leaders of all Denominations and non-Denominational churches. These leaders they will not like it when someone is talking about them, and especially when it is "harsh words". As far as I see it, they are doing a lousy job in the last 40 to 50 years, and most of the attendants in these congregations do not even know the name of these leaders anyway. My goal is to shake up these born-again churches all around the world. Personally, I cannot remove the veil in the front of your eyes, and God cannot remove it either, it has to be you, and only you, who can do it. Jesus didn't come in here to start a denomination. He came to tell mankind to abolish all religion on this earth, and replace it with His Teaching called "THE WAY", and it is a NO, NO, to all who are religious, people do not want to let go of their religion, it became sacred to them. (How can it be sacred when it comes from the devil?). Many born-again Christians seams that they have lost their first Love, the answer is that they didn't lose it, they actually "LET IT SLIDE", and become sleepy because of the preacher easy-peasy when he speaks and acts week after week. Do not take it personally, guys, I am talking to the world in general. I do not know you or your church, so how can I talk about you personally, when I do not know you? Look in Revelation chapters 2 and 3 and read it slowly, and you will find out that these churches that the angel was naming are actually the churches in the future, in the end time, or close to it. These churches they do not have a denomination name, because it was written 1900 years ago (AD 100).

Some of these churches did not come alive some 500 years and some 1500 years later, so you really have to read these chapters with your eyeglasses of Faith. Out of 7 churches (Denomination), only one was faithful. Is it what Jesus will find when He returns and finds faithless churches (6 of 7 churches)? Do not forget that these churches are alive today with a denominational name. When you are reading it with your eyeglasses of Faith, these two chapters are speaking about us (now). There is only one thing before the rapture is to come, and it is the peace treaty that Israel will sign with his nemesis. Also, Israel does not believe that Jesus was (and is) the Son of God, and they are waiting for Him to come. And when you are reading John 5:43, Jesus said, "I have come in My Father's Name, and you do not receive Me, when another comes in his own name, him you will receive." Outch.

Now listen to this: some of you who do not want to follow God's Word because He is too strict. Except, you might believe in him who will come in his own name ministry, and he will be gentle, and will be speaking soft word to you. Be aware of a wolf disguised in sheep's clothing. This is what will happen with the Jewish people when they will sign that treaty and believing that this man is their savior. Outch! I did not come to attack one Denomination; I came to attack them all—at once. Be aware also of religious people. Most of these Denominational churches do not want to lose their power in this world; they want to be bigger and bigger than the one who is bigger than them. It is also about $$$$$$$$$$$$-very important to them. Jesus said this is "THE WAY" that I want you to follow, not a religion or a Denomination; I want you to follow Me. So, lots of time born-again Christians will follow the one who came with his own name ministry ---him you will receive. OUtCH!

"False words do not bear fruits." (Sophocles 1)

Be careful what's coming out of your mouth---period.

Words that we speak are the most powerful thing in the universe. Your tongue can be a destructive way in your life, and also words correctly speak it can be a powerful force in your Life. Mark 11:24, Jesus said: Therefore, I say to you, "**almost**" everything you ask when you believe that you did receive them, and you will have them. (I added the word **almost** because there is something that God cannot do sometimes. When you pray for something that is contrary to His Word that He has already spoken, He cannot give it to you, because He has to break His Word, and He will not do that just to please you. It is why I said **almost** everything, you ask). So, now you have to know His Law (Word) before you speak to Him, even when you desire to receive, He cannot give it to you. God is a Spirit living in the Spirit World (Fourth dimension), and it is controlled by His Words---the Word of God. His Words are Spiritual Law in the universe. His policy is that His Words will become a Spiritual Force working with you, and for you. So, your own words can be against you when you speak contrary to His Words. When you open your mouth to say your **special prayer (or request),** be careful what you are saying, because God already said that you will receive when you do believe with all your heart what you are saying to Him. Did your preacher tell you about "How a Thanksgiving prayer works"? Did he tell you how precisely how it works? Did he tell you that it is very important for you to know about that? Sometimes when we did not receive **yet** we wonder, and you will say with your mouth **it doesn't work** or **I can't seem to get rid of my problem** or it looks like that my problem is getting worse than before (Because you are impatient). So, you are asking God**, why** did I not receive it yet. God will say to you: Who told you that it doesn't work? And you will remember that the voice in your head did say; it doesn't work, and you decided to believe that voice in your head, who is your enemy, and you decided on your own to speak the same thing that you heard. The voice in your head it is not God's voice, and it is not Satan either; it is a demon working for him because Satan cannot be everywhere at once. When God do speak to us, He speaks in our heart, not in our head, because God is everywhere at once. (Omnipresent). God will say to you: "No-wonder you did not receive, you are speaking the words of your enemy". What I say to you is, start to believe that you already did receive, and thou shalt receive it later. You do know that I **God,** also say that it is impossible for Me to lie, so, I Am telling the truth then. When I say to you to give Me your problem, and I will take care of it, it will become My problem, and not yours anymore so, let Me handle it because I already know the answer (Trust as to go both ways). What you should do is to continue to believe **Him,** not him. Thanksgiving prayers are the second most important thing that you should do for you to receive. Don't forget your spoken words, that you did give it to Him, let Him handle it, because it is His problem from now on, not yours. Thanksgiving prayer is to say thank You, Father, I do know that You already did find the answer, and I believe that it has already been solved, thank you Father. As a born-again, you already know how to finish your prayer (Or your request) in Jesus, name. When you say Thanksgiving prayers, you do not say, In Jesus name when you finish that Thanksgiving prayer, you just say Thank You, Father. These prayers are just 10 to 15-second prayers anyway. So, just say it to Him 4 to 5 times a day, and continue to believe that it is already yours. When you say to yourself, and to Him, "it doesn't work," you are absolutely right; it will not work. You cannot pray the problem, you do have from now on, know that to pray the answer, that is actually the answer. Saying it 4 to 5 times a day is a good number; it's not because you will say it 60 times a day that you will receive it faster. You cannot make it to come faster, this is not how it works. Repetitive words are not the way to receive faster, you cannot "force it" to come. What you have to do is to believe it, with all your heart, not with all your mind. The world told us to believe with all your minds, and many preachers are preaching it, and they don't even know that they are speaking the same way as the world speaks, because they do not pay attention to their own words. This is why I decided to write this book: **Be careful what's coming out of your mouth.**

Most of the time, we (The entire human being), as far as I know, we do not pay attention to what we are saying, we just saying it, and that's it. Preachers are human too, and they do make mistakes sometimes, so, do not be too hard on them, we all speak the words of the enemy, and we don't even know it. Ex: Come here for one second, can I borrow your pen for one second, I'll be there in one second, we know that it will take more than one second, only we decided to tell a lie instead of telling the truth. We should say instead, Can I borrow your pen for a few minutes. When a commentator on television saw something that a player did, and it was a great play, the commentator would say, "I don't believe it". He saw the play, and the camera will show it again in slow motion, the commentator will still continue to say that he doesn't believe it when he knew for a fact that the player did catch the ball, and instead of saying the truth, he will tell a lie. He should tell the truth, and say, wow, what a catch, and I am happy that I did see it with my own eyes, because it will be very hard to believe it, only I did see it, wow, what a play. So, he is lying to 10 million people, and he doesn't even know that he is doing it. 2 Corinthians 5:7, Paul said: For we walk by Faith, not by sight, and I Normand is saying to you that you should, and have to walk by Faith, and not by what you are seeing. You cannot pray contrary as His Word said, you have to follow His directive Words. Also, you have to think like Him, talk like Him.

Act like Him. He already said to us, "Be like Me".

"A man/woman who lies to themselves, and believes their own lies, become unable to recognize the truth, either in themselves or in anyone else" (Fyodor 1821-1881)

God's Word is "Spiritual Law", and we men (Human) have our own law, it is called "Natural law". When Righteous people are using God's Words when we are speaking, we are speaking the truth. When natural people speak Satan's words (As the world speaks), they are not speaking the truth, because there is no truth in Satan's words. Satan does not like it when people, especially born-again people, speak God's Word; he wants you to speak his words, and his words only. Sometimes we, born-again we speak the word of the devil, without knowing it, and we are speaking it the same way as the world speaks (Even me sometime I make mistakes, and speak his words by old habits, and when I am hearing myself of what I just said, I correct myself right away). James 3:8-10, No man/woman can tame the tongue, it is an unruly evil, full of deadly poison. With it we bless our God and Father, and with it we curse men/women who have been made in the similitude of God. Out of the same mouth proceeds Blessing and cursing. My brothers/sisters, these things ought not to be so. James 1:26, When anyone thinks he/she is religious (Righteous), and does not bridle his/her tongue, and deceives his/her own heart (Lie to oneself), this one's religion (Righteousness) is useless. I did change these two words religious and religion for "Righteous and Righteousness", because we, born-again believers we do not have a religion, because we are not religious. So, to the one who is reading these Gospels, and has a religion, be aware of what you are reading as a full proof Gospel, because I suspect that these bad theologians did put their dirty fingers of religion into that statement of James, and put it according to the way that their doctrine sees it. Matthew 12:37, "For by your words you will be justified, and by your words you will be condemned". So, your own words will actually be the ones who will be judging you (Your own words), and nobody put these words in your heart by force; you, yourself, choose to say it the way you did. (Before it comes out of your mouth, you have to put them in your heart) So, your word can be a blessing or a curse when it comes out of your mouth, Wow!

I better to be careful about everything I say from now on, and you might say to yourself, "I should be watching my own words and when someone speaks, to really pay attention, the way they say it. Is it true what that person said? Is it a factual fact? Maybe I should check it out more closely before I start to believe everything I read and hear. When you can control your tongue, you will be in control of your entire body, and when you don't, it can destroy you, and bring you in the gutter's or it can build an empire for you in your life. When you choose your words carefully and act on it, and really believe what you are saying is true, and it is on its way, then you will find out that your own words can be as powerful as God's Words. God did say, "Be like Me". God's Words are powerful Words. God's Words can create. God's Words can destroy His enemies. (Satan is already defeated, except he is still doing lots of damage to God's people, it is just a matter of time before he will be locked down for 1000 years. I can wait; I'm going nowhere. **Almost** every Words of God are Faith Words, and when I talk like Him, act like Him, and believe like Him, how can I lose? Its impossible for me to lose. I can create my own future in my life, and for the future after I die. When you die its over, we cannot change anything, so I will suggest to you to be very aware of that, because too late is too late. You can ask God to take care of your enemy, and all that you have to do is to believe that you are free of them by Faith, and that you will be free. You might even start to sing that beautiful song.

Soon very soon I will be, and will be free--Yeah

Soon very soon I will be, and will be free—Yeah

Soon very soon I will be, free from my enemy

Alleluia, alleluia, I'm free from my enemy.

Your words are the most powerful things in your universe, so have fun with it, you have nothing to lose, and have all to gain when you really believe these words. You can speak them or you can sing them, what do you have to lose? When your heart is happy, your whole body will be healthy. You can have everything that you are asking as long that it is according, or not interfere with God's Law. When a person who does not receive, it is most likely a lack of knowledge. When the leaders at the top of your Denomination do not "Groom" their preachers to become teachers and to teach his congregation, well, I will tell you that everyone loses in that church. You become the biggest loser, and your preacher becomes a loser in the eyes of God. These leaders at the top they will have to pay for what they didn't do when they were capable. Laziness sometimes it is hard to detect, and God can do it, because He is the only One who can read your heart, and your thoughts (Mind), leaders be aware of that. So, when your words do not match from what you are thinking or what you have in your heart, He will know. Laziness settles in, and it is hard to get rid of, especially when it is there for a long time.

"I'm not upset that you lie to me, I'm upset

that from now on I can't believe you."

(Frederick 1844---1900)

Hosea 4:6, God is speaking against Israel, who did remove God from them hearts, and put a religion instead, and this is what He said in verse 6: "My people (Jews and Gentiles) are destroyed by lack of knowledge. John the Baptist was the last Prophet of God, just before Jesus was, and John the Baptist had the Spirit of God since his mother's womb. Jesus Himself said that John was the greatest Prophet of all, and since John and Jesus, there is no Prophet for the last 1992 years so far in Israel. The people in Israel do not even ask themselves the question, "Why" is it that God did not send a Prophet in the land of Israel His peoples? Their eyes of religion do not make them possible for them to see that they crucified the Son of God; Who was the Son of Man. This is why today they walk by sight, and not by Faith. Jesus, in His Teaching to the elders of Israel, He told them: "You do not believe My Words that I Am the Son of God and later (When the antichrist comes) you will believe the voice of a man, and believe that he is your savior, and you will make peace with him. In 8 years from now, it will be 2000 years since His resurrection, and the rapture might (I emphasize the word might) take place then, and they will make peace with that "fake savior", and 3 ½ years later, you will see his true nature--- outch. (In 2033? you might see the shit hit the fan -- outch). Daniel 9:27, Then he (The antichrist) shall confirm a covenant with many (Nations) for one week (7 years), and in the middle of the week (3

1/2years later), he shall bring an end of sacrifice and offering. There is more---on the wing of desolations shall be one who makes desolate, even until the consummation which is determined, is poured out of the desolate. Daniel 12:11, "From the time that the daily sacrifice is taken away, and the abomination of desolation is set up, there shall be 1290 days", and this is when the Jewish people will recognize their mistake, and their eyes will be open--- that's another outch. All this will happen because of "Lack of knowledge", and this will continue to all the Gentile churches, up to now also. People are suffering because of "Lack of knowledge". This is why the born-again churches should have someone who teaches the Word of God, and notpreaches it. Jesus said that you should ask the Holy Spirit when He will come (He did 1992 years ago) to receive the Gift of the Spirit. The Gift of teaching is a Gift from God, and when you haven't received that Gift yet, Jesus said that you can ask for it. Jesus He is the Door for your salvation, and to all religious churches, you will have to go with what your religion offered you to have your salvation---and it is "NOTHING". Jesus is the only way; it is not your religion or Denomination that will save you. He is the only way to enter the Kingdom of Heaven. Everyone has to go through Him, not by worshipping idols, or some other god, or by sacrifice and hard work. The only way is with your mouth. It is so simple, you open your mouth and ask Him to come into your heart as your personal Savior, and to believe it with all your heart. It is so simple that people have a hard time believing how easy it is. So, they are saying to themselves, it must be a catch because it is too easy. Most likely they choose the "hard way" ---religion instead, and My people are destroyed for "Lack of knowledge". Jesus said: My people (Born-again) do not receive because they do not know how to ask. Luke 11:2, When you pray, **say.** He never said when you pray in your head (In silence), He said: "**say**". So, now you will have to open your mouth from now on. You say your own prayer using your own words, and believe it what you are saying with all your heart. You do not say the "Lord's prayer"; that prayer is not yours, because it is not your own. It was Jesus' prayer; it was His own. That special prayer when He said to the Apostles to pray was before the Resurrection; today, you cannot say that prayer because it will not help you to receive. (**It's the Lord prayer, not yours**) You are using your own words that come from your heart, and believe that you have already received what you are saying or asking, and it becomes **your** special prayer **at that moment**. It is a personal prayer to you; it is not somebody else prayer that you pray, it is your own. When you are using your own words and asking for your body to be healed, you do not say a prayer to thank Him for your new job.

When you need help from God for whatever you need from Him, Ex: you are looking for a job, or be free from a bully at school, or are looking for a spouse to share your life, you will go nowhere with the Lord's prayer, and the simple explanation, it is not your own, it is the Lord's prayer. When you need to pray and want to receive, start using your own words, and God who looks in your heart to see how much you believe in what's coming out of your mouth, continue to believe that it is already yours, and thou shall receive according to your heart. I will repeat what Jesus said: **My people do not receive because they do not know how to ask**. Now, you know how to ask---just do it, its easy.

"A lie can travel halfway around the world while the truth is putting on its shoes"

(Samuel Clemens 1835—1910)

John 16:23, Jesus said: In that day (After His Resurrection) you will ask Me nothing. This is why that the people do not receive, because 1992 years later, people are still asking Him something, and this distinguishes readers, **it is a full lack of knowledge,** and the leaders of your Denomination, and the preachers also are to blame for that "lack of knowledge". You cannot blame no other, they are responsible when their sheep are not walking strongly in the Lord. When you pray, you ask God (Not Jesus), and at the same time that you are praying your own words, you hear them---right, and you know that you are not a liar, and when you are hearing your own words, you will believe them because you are not a liar---right. When you are hearing your own truth coming out of your mouth, it will be easy for you to believe them, and God did say that they will go into your heart, because this is where that you believe in your heart, not in your head, or mind. When you finish that special prayer (Any prayer is special to Him), you said to God: I am asking this in Jesus Name (Amen is not necessary, only it makes a nice touch, and personally I am using it). I will tell you something, supposing that you are not born-again, you cannot finish your prayer in Jesus Name. Well you can, only it will not work, because Jesus He is not your personal Savior. It doesn't mean that you are praying for nothing, this is not what I am saying---not at all. Now listen carefully, God did say to us (Human beings) that when you pray, and believe with all your heart, "thou shalt receive" what you are asking for.

God didn't say; that when you believe with all your heart, and you have to be born again, then you will receive. No, no, no, no, no, He said: to whomever believes with all their heart, "You will receive". That you are in a religion or not, it doesn't matter, we will all receive. As for you who do not believe that God exists, it makes no difference to Him, He cannot come back on His Word and give it to the person who believes in Him only. Most likely, the one who do not believe in Him they will pray to the universe and ask what they want, because they know it works. It is not you who did choose God; it is He who did choose you. He started to love you before your conception, so, now you can see He loves you first. It's great to hear how great He is. Every human being, when praying to God or to the universe, we did receive that same answer: "Thou shalt receive what you are asking for," and you will receive according to your own heart, and when you don't receive, it is because you did not believe it with all your heart, it is very simple. Faith and doubt do not work; hand in hand, be aware of that. That kind of teaching, you will never hear this in a born-again church, that you can believe. We born-again people say sometimes: God is good all the time, all the time God is good. The unbelievers will probably say: the universe is good all the time, all the time the universe is good. Now, let's continue. After you finish your prayer, what should you do? The answer is easy. Just sit and wait, play a game of chess, or read a book, and wait for that answer from God or the universe---yeah, just wait.

I am joking people do not do that.

I just put myself in trouble is in it, and people will be mad. It was not exactly a joke; it was a lie disguised as a joke. Do you see how easy it is to lie, and no one saw it, it was disguised. So, after you finish your request or your prayer, start the second step. You will have to open your mouth and say prayers of Thanksgiving when you are a believer. As for the unbelievers, start to say thank you to the universe, after all, it is the most powerful ATM you have ever believed in, and you might even say I can have almost anything from that ATM---Wow. So, start to say thanks to whom you believe, and speak it 4 to 5 times a day (It's a good number). Continue to say these prayers of Thanksgiving up to the time that you will receive. Did you see I did say prayers, not prayer, so, continue to believe with all your heart, and when you decided to listen to the voice in your head, that say: it doesn't work, and when you will say it with your mouth, well, you will not receive I can tell you that, because you do believe that "it doesn't work". Now listen to a "Fictional story." Two persons, wherever they are in the world, they do not know each other, and they might even speak a different language, and they both pray the same prayer or request to God (Or the universe). They are praying the same prayer on the same day. They are both very busy with their life (Job, kid(s), etc.) One of the two will say a Thanksgiving prayer at least 5 times a day. Busy or not, he/she will take time to say a few words for 3 to 15 seconds, because that person really wants it to come faster. The second person is busy too, only he/she did not get my memo, and decided to say one prayer a day, when he/she goes to bed. They both continue to believe that they did receive it by Faith, what they did ask. One month passed, and the person who was praying 5 times a day did receive it, and what a joy---right. The other person will not receive it at the same time, because the first one did pray 5 times a day, compared to praying one time a day. So, when the second person continues to say one prayer a day, and continues to believe with all his/her heart, that person will finally receive in about 5 months. (1x5=5) Now this is why I am telling you that fictional story, because I want you to hear this: **How badly that you want it to come?** It is up to you to decide how bad you want it to come. Don't forget that lack of knowledge is not good. Your heart is a "Garden" where you will plant your "seed" (Prayer or request). In, let's say a week later, with your eyes of Faith, you are looking in your heart to see your seed that you did plant. Looking in, you'll see that there is a little tige that came out from the ground, and you will say, and using your mouth (It's very important), wow, my seed is now dead, and it became a plant--- alright. So, now when you do it like that, it will help you to believe that it is working, it is on its way. There are so many things that we can do to help ourselves to continue to believe that it is on its way. This is why it is so important that you say many times a day, because every time you say thanks, you are putting water on your plant. You can see it now, the difference between 1, 3, 5, 7 times that you water your plant that you can receive it 3,5,7, times faster. That's up to you, don't go and blame whoever you think he/she is responsible. Look in the mirror, and you see the answer right in front of you. Outch, that one hurts. It is not as easy as you think it is to receive. It demands work---from you. You will have to work at it, and continue to believe, and believe, and believe. One of the saddest things to say is that people are too lazy to do all that "hard work". Laziness is one of the downfalls of the born-again Christians, or to the one who believe in the ATM. Don't be lazy, do the work. This is why they do not receive--yet. Unless your preacher does not know it, and he cannot preach something he doesn't know in the first place.

"There are always 4 sides of a story: your side, their side, the truth and what really happened"

(Jean Jacques Rousseau) (1712—1778)

So, let's go back to our steps, and how to do to succeed, and pray to the Father (Or universe), and say it with your mouth. Step 1: Ask the Father (Not Jesus) or the universe, and use your mouth. Step 2/3: At the same time that you are hearing your own words, start to believe with all your heart that you have already did receive it. Step 4: As a born-again, finish your prayer in Jesus Name. As an unbeliever (Of God), just say: I know it is on its way. Step 5: Say Thanksgiving prayers 4 to 5 times a day, when you do wants to receive faster, and to the unbelievers, just continue to say thanks. Step 6: Do not stop believing until you receive. Step 7: Rejoice, you just did receive today---rejoice indeed. The more you are using your Faith, you'll see, it will become easier and easier for you to continue to believe, and your Faith will become "Stronger". Words are little seeds that produce after their kind. You will reap what you sow. For all of you who are lazy, I will say to you: Keep your mouth shut, and I am telling you that there will be no harvest either. I know I have been to some of your churches, some people do not use their mouth to pray, they pray in their head, and they don't even sing either with their mouth (They sing in their head). This is the God that you will be worshipping in Heaven. Is it the same God that you will sing songs in Heaven, because you will be forced to do it? Continue to read my book, and you will find out; that you, Sir, Ma'am, will most likely be a knocker. It is never too late to change for the better. There is another thing that church people will never hear someone preaching in their churches, that the devil's words are powerful too. I don't recall ever hearing someone preaching on that subject---ever. God's Words are as much powerful today than yesterday and 4500 years ago. His Words does not change, they do not become weaker than before, and are not stronger than before, they are and stay the same today and yesterday. Try to explain that to a theologian; good luck with that, because every 150 years or so, they come out with another Bible to rewrite, and they are saying: "We will not change the meaning or Words of God," and when you are reading God speaking, it doesn't sound the same. I despised that trade (Theology) with a passion. Let's go back to teaching. The words of the devil are powerful, only when you believe them. Ex: When people say: I don't believe it, it's impossible, God does not exist, I am sick, etc.

These words are powerful to whom who believe them, and to the one who do not believe these words (Devil words), they mean absolutely nothing to us. This is why it is so crucial that you pay attention to what's coming out of your mouth. These theologians they don't, they just babble. The way to notice these words is for you to listen to them in the first place, with your outside ears. We all one time or another, speak the words of the devil; it's just that we don't even know it, because we do not pay attention to our own words when we speak. When someone says to his/her co-worker: I can't wait to go on vacation, and that person will say, I thought that you would be going only in two weeks from now. So, the person will answer, Oh! I am it just that I can't wait? Are you going now or wait? No, I will wait. Why do you say you can't wait when you can then? Well, it is just a way to speak, you know---you know what I mean. No, I don't know what you mean. I only know what you said. Why not tell it like it is: I know that my vacation is not before two weeks, except that I am anxious to go now, only I will have to wait. We speak the words of the devil since we are 3 years old, and it is not easy to change the way we speak. It cannot be done in an instant, it takes time because we have spoken that language for so long, and it is not easy because of our old habits when we speak that language for 20 or 90 years. There are so many expressions that we say and hear for so long that come from the devil. The devil does not want us to speak the truth, this is why he made people 6000 years ago to start to speak his own words. We speak his lie over and over every day, and we don't even notice that. This is why that God said that every man (Woman also) is a liar. The devil found a way to "Slide" hypocrite Lý in our language of everyday, and it was subtle, and now we have to be careful what's coming out of our mouths. When we speak the same way that God speaks, we know that we are telling the truth. Some of you might think that this teaching of mine it is stupid, and you are right, it is stupid---to you, not to me. When you speak the truth, God will notice the change and will be there to help you to achieve it faster. It is not because you hear this for the first time that I am telling you lies. You might even say to yourself, I don't like the way he speaks, only, I didn't hear him telling fibs.

"A lie told often enough becomes the truth" (Brainwashing)

(Vladimir Lenin) (1870—1924)

This is a true story of when I was living in Las Vegas, Nevada. One time our preacher in Las Vegas asked for volunteers to fill it the crack in the asphalt parking lot for next Saturday. So, lots of peoples shows up, and we start working, and it happens that I have a shovel in my hands, and the preacher said to me: Normand, can I borrow your shovel for one second, I say yes. So, I give it to him, and one second later I took it back from his hand, and he said: What you doing, and I said to him, you said just for one second, and he said: well, it is for a couple minutes, and I said to him, why did you not say a couples of minutes then. He said, you know what I mean, I said No, I do not know what you mean. I only know what you said. I give him back the shovel, and a couple of minutes later, he gives it back to me. This happened just before COVID, when it hit everywhere in the world all at once. After COVID, when we were able to travel, I did make it back to Canada, and I never saw my preacher before I left. So, today I am wondering, did he learn something? (I do not know) How many times in your live that you heard someone say: "You know what I mean"? Are we capable of reading someone mind or reading inside their heart? NO, only, we can guess though. Why not tell the truth then? It's so simple? When you know for a fact that it will take 3minutes, why say one second then? So, instead of telling the truth, you decide to tell a lie, is it easier????? The famous answer that people respond with is: That's the way we speak. So, even my preacher was speaking the same way as the world speaks, and he did not even know it. We have to be careful not to comfort into that same language that the world speaks. It is not easy though, and we have to work at it, and most of the peoples will not do it, because it is too much work, laziness it is something that God despised the most, He doesn't like it when someone is lazy. He still likes you; only, He despised your action that is a non-action. He doesn't like a person who just stands and does Nothing. They there are 7 ways for you to decide what to do. Imagine that you are standing on the third floor of a five-story building. There are stairs and elevators for you to go up or down, there are offices all around you, also. You are standing, and waiting which direction to choose to go in your life, and it happens that only one is the right way to do, as far as God is concerned. Later in life, you might change direction. God is ok with that because He already gave us choices to choose. You can go forward, or turn around in the other direction, you can go to your left, or to your right, or go down in the elevator to the lower story, or go up in the elevator to the fourth story. So, you can see that there are 6 ways (For now) that you can actually go in your life. One of the six ways is the right way, and you are not sure which one is the best for your own life. You might know that God's way will be the perfect way for you, only you are not ready to go that way---yet. The seventh way is to just to "stand", and for some people probably the one, they will choose, is to just stand and do nothing with in their life.

When you did choose one way, God is good with that, because He gave us choices for us to choose. When you are going the wrong way, He kind of accepts it, at least you are moving into one direction that you think it is the best for you. This is how the Holy Spirit showed it to me. Laziness is "Almost" a sin to God. I put it this way: **He cannot stand it** to see someone just stand and do nothing. You might be going in the wrong direction right now, but at least you are moving; you are not just standing. Who knows, you might become one of His Child, in the near future, I can't say, and you can't say it either, only He knows.

"When you tell the truth
you don't have to remember anything"
(Samuel Clemens)
(1835---1910)

When you are thinking right, and you will act on your thinking, you will be right. When you are thinking wrong, and you will act on your thinking, you will be wrong. When you are thinking stupidly, and you will be acting on your stupidity, you will be stupid. It is all about the "Thinking", that you are right, or wrong, or stupid. When you sow Righteousness, or evilness, or wickedness, you will reap what you sow. You can speak the Word of God the same way that Abraham did, and 3500 years later, they will work for you. When you will be using the devil words, they will work against you, though.

So, be careful what's coming out of your mouth.

God, when He decided to create the Heavens and the Earth, He did use His own Words, "After all" it is His world. We, as living beings we can create our own limited universe also, to fit our own life, and using our own words. You do not need to believe in God to receive what you are asking (It is better when you do, though). You can create your own future to a certain point, and even when God does not approve, He cannot come back on His Word and change it. That you believe in Him or not, it makes no difference, His Word has already out there for 6000 years and counting, and His Word will stay the same. God did say that when you will ask, and believe with all your heart that you will receive according to your heart. Not according to your political party, to your denomination leaders, to your spouse, to your boss, to your preacher, to your neighbor, or your family, no, He said according to your heart. This is why I said to all of you, you do not need to be a born-again only for you to receive. As long that you yourself believe what you are saying to yourself, and believe with all your heart well "Thou shalt receive". The unbelievers who are very successful, they really believe in their own words, and they succeed daily, and us who are born-again and have God in us; why is it that the unbelievers are more successful than us? When you live your life and you have never heard much about God, to you, He does not exist. They do not have the fear of God; sin is not really something that it is on your mind. Shame is not much a part in your thoughts a lot, or feeling guilty of something you did to someone. Most likely, they will not say these expressions: It doesn't work, I can't believe it, I am afraid, etc. Evil will not come and put a stick on their wheel when they are creating their own future. The voice that we born-again heard often in our head to try to make us do something unrighteous, or bothering us with these thoughts, like it doesn't work, well, them they do not have a problem as much as us believers. They know about karma, it is a part of the universe where they do their "Shopping", they are not sure how it works, only that it works. They know it exists, and that you can speak to it, and receive what its on their "Shopping list". That kind of teaching will never be preached in so many churches; you can be sure of that. WHO IS THE HYPOCRITE THEN. I personally decided to use my mouth and my pen to do something about that. I will not be standing and doing nothing, like so many leaders do. The unbelievers are not necessarily doing evil because they have never heard about Him. They live their life the way they see fit from the teachings they receive since their youth. You cannot do evil when evil is not in your mind. Hosea 4:6, My people are destroyed for "Lack of knowledge." So, Normand will paraphrase Hosea 4:6, My brothers and sisters in the Lord are destroyed because their leaders keep them in the dark, or keep them blindfolded. It's the best way for them to control who they want to control, keep them in the dark, misinform, and Normand will continue to say it like it is that My people are destroyed for "Lack of knowledge" even in 2025. You might be mad at me, and I will say to you, "Take a number" and you are not the first. Some will say: I do not like the way he speaks, only he didn't lie once. At least Normand he is not standing and doing nothing. This is how I see it. God did open His mouth and said: "Light be", and the sun, moon, and stars all appeared in the universe. He did it with something that we cant see, "Words", and God said, "Be like me" The unbelievers, without knowing what God says, they act the same way He did. They are doing it the right way, and they don't even know it, that they are doing it the same way as God intended for us to do also. God created the universe with His own Word, and the universe came into existence.

Unbelievers believe in their own words, and with the limited Faith that they have, they manage to receive (Almost) everything they say, because they believe their own words with all their heart. You know that I am right saying all this, because you can see that they are quite more successful than us born-again. The question that born- again have on their lips is: How come they are more successful than us born-again Christians? Now you know the answer.

"When people cannot change things, they change the words"

(Jean Jaurès) (1859--1914

Charles Capps said: FAITH WILL MAKE PRAYER WORK, AND PRAYER WON'T MAKE FAITH WORK. FAITH WILL WORK WITHOUT PRAYER---PRAYER WON'T WORK WITHOUT FAITH.

All the unbelievers they are all doing it the right way, and they might not know how it works, only that they know it works the way that they are doing it. They will continue doing it the same way because they know "It works", and God cannot stop them from receiving, because He cannot break His own Words. God's Words are already out there for anyone to follow them, and by now, the entire world knows that words are the most powerful thing in the universe. You can create something with them, and you can destroy your enemy with them. Words are invisible, and you can do something with them---or create something. **Don't just "stand there," do something with them.** God created the living being to "Imitate Him", and to operate their Faith as He does it Himself---with His Faith. After all, we were created in the image (Likeness) of God. It is understandable for us, the believers, to imitate our Father (God), and the unbelievers to imitate their father (Satan). One thing that I want you to know is, as a born-again believer (Today), your first father was the devil. I understand that you did do the switch, from father to Father. I know by listening to some of you that we born-again sometimes speak like the world speaks, and the devil is the father of all who were born on this earth with Adam's blood in them (I am happy I did do the switch). The unbelievers obviously do not know God; only, they speak like Him (To a certain point), act like Him (Using Faith Words), and when it is time to ask the universe (God) something, they already know about believing and such, and one thing they will not do is; to talk like their father. Ex: They will never say: it doesn't work, or I don't believe it, etc. (Because they know it works). They will use words from a God; Who does not exist (To them), and will not follow the words of their own father, the devil (We have very, very strange people living on this planet is in it). God said: "He/she shall have whatsoever what he/she said." Whether you believe in Him or not, God He is saying to anyone, follow My steps (Believers or unbelievers). I will paraphrase what God is saying to us. Let's all do it together with our Faith, and imitate Me. God wants us to believe with all our hearts. The devil wants us to believe with all our minds. When you believe with all your heart when God did say that; this is where it will go---in your heart. The devil wants you to believe with all your mind, and this is where it will go---in your mind. Personally, I believe that when someone believes with all his/her mind, to me it sounds like a "fart". When you speak or do a fart, you did hear it---right! So, to me, it is just like a "fart", you heard it, and now it is gone. This is why I am writing this book; it is for you to know that when you speak the words of the devil, and believe his words, ex: It doesn't work, and you believe it that it doesn't work, you just did put these words of the devil in your heart, and you don't even know it.

BE AWARE OF WHAT'S COMING OUT OF YOUR MOUTH---PERIOD.

Galatians 6:9, Let us not grow weary while doing good, for in due season we shall reap, **when** we do not lose heart 1 Corinthians 3:5-9, Who then is Paul, and who is Apollos, although ministers through whom you believed, as the Lord gave to each one? I planted, Apollos watered, and God gave the Increase. So then neither he who plants is anything, nor he who waters, nevertheless it is God who gives the Increase. Now he who plants and he who waters are one, and each one will receive his own reward according to his own labor. For we are God's fellow workers; you are God's field, and you are God's building. We are a member of the body of Christ, so we cannot do all by ourselves, sometime people do not give the credit to whom the credit should be awarded, and they take the whole credit for themselves. Now that you have read these verses, I personally want to be fair to anyone who are those "Fellow workers", so I decided to rewrite these verses 5-9, so that it will be fair to anyone who are those workers.

Normand version of 1 Corinthians 3:5-9.

Who then is Paul, and who is Apollos (It is you and me---right), and ministers through Whom you believed, as the Lord Gave to each one? I planted,

17

Apollos watered, and God "Gave the Increase." So, neither he/she who plants is anything, nor he/she who waters are one, and each one will receive his/her reward according to his/her own labor. For we are God's "Fellow workers"; you are God's field (His Child), you are God's building (Your body is the Temple of the Holy Spirit). Can you see now that every born-again is a "Fellow worker". To me, it is important to give credit to anyone who earns it. FAIR IS FAIR.

When I was a few months into my new Faith, I really have a hard time for me to understand Romans 10:17, So, then Faith comes by hearing, and hearing the Word of God. I didn't understand why that Paul as to be using the word "hearing" twice in that sentence. Most likely the Holy Spirit want it to be saying exactly like that? Personally, I will have it written like this: "Faith comes by hearing the Word of God." Because we men we know something about "short-cut" ---right. It will be simple to read and understand---am I right? Let's take a vote. (I do believe that I will lose my vote) So, this verse did bother me for a long time, and one day I asked God about it, and today I know "Why", because He did give me the answer 18 years later. I didn't remember that "Request" that I made to Him, only that I found out that the Holy Spirit was preparing me for my future, and today I can see it now, all the work of the Holy Spirit step by step, did for me to learn "Why" that the word "Hearing" was mention twice in that sentence. In July 1985, I did move from Quebec, Canada, to Ontario, Canada, and I had to start to learn a new language (To me) at 31 years of age. I will have to learn American English. I didn't want to learn English, because I will have to go to England. So, I opted for American English, it is the language they spoke in most Canada anyway (Short-cut remember). 18 years later, I was reading a book about Faith by Charles Capps (1934- 2014) about Romans 10:17, and I did find the answer in Charles book that I was looking for 18 years earlier. You see, I had to learn English to be able to know the answer because that book was not translated into theFrench language.

What a joy when I finally got to read that answer I was looking—for so long. The author of the book "**The tongue a creative force**" was telling us; why that Paul had to say it that way. "Faith comes by hearing, and hearing the Word of God." He (Charles) said: This is how you should read that verse. "Faith comes by hearing, and hearing, and hearing, and hearing, and hearing, and hearing, and hearing---the Word of God." What a joy to finally be able to understand that beautiful answer from Charles. Now I understand why I had to move to Ontario, Canada, and learn English first, so that I will be able to receive my answer to my request 18 years earlier. In those 18 years gap, I made a few mistakes along my route. I got married to a "fake Christian lady", outch, that one hurts. I did move to the good old USA in 1994, and became a US citizen in 1996, and in 2004, I decided to leave my spouse (A chronic liar), and I decided to became homeless from 2004 to 2011. What a beautiful time I did have, as a homeless person. Well; almost all the time. Today, when I look at my decision to move to Ontario, Canada, now I know that the Holy Spirit has something to do with that, and He put the right people on my path. When I was a teenager, I was looking at books, and magazines (National Geographic) that we had at home, and I was looking at pictures of Las Vegas. It became one of my goals, growing up, to move over there. Working in the construction in Quebec in winter was not fun. I was saying to my co-workers that I will not stay here all my life, you can make sure of that. When I was 12 years old, our mother, who was more Catholic than the Pope, and during school day, she woke us up at 6:15 am for us to go to the ½ hr. mass. One time when I was listening to the crow, who was speaking in front, (The crow is the priest because he is wearing a black robe) and I was hearing him saying: "You have to be Catholic to go to Heaven." My mind started to wonder about the children my age in Russia and China, and that their leaders do not allow any religion in their country. All these children are the same age as me, they will have no chances for them to go in Heaven. I was saying in my mind: why is it that me, and I was putting my right hand on my heart, and repeating why me, why me? Why was I so lucky to be born in a Catholic family? Why me, why I was so lucky? It was the Holy Spirit Who was working around me (The Spirit of God was not in me yet), how come I was so, so lucky to be born in Canada, not in China. I did find the "complete" answer to my question---why me? It did take me 54 years or so. From 12 of age, when I started to "Wonder about things," God was keeping an eye on me. I didn't know that at the time, except that today I can see it. I enjoy homelessness in summers 1974 and 1976, when I was hitchhiking in Canada it was a preparation for my future life, which will come toward me in about 50 years later (Was born in 1954 +50= 2004).

When I decided to leave my spouse, it was because of her lies and the fact that she tried to put me in jail for no reason whatsoever. She lost in court because of all her lies, they didn't fit, and at that moment I decided to become homeless. I already knew what it was to live on the street, and I did love it, so I said to myself, let's go. I said to my soon-to-be ex. that she can keep everything, I do not need money, and when I will need money, I know Who to ask, indicating God with my index finger, and I became homeless in 2004 in Toledo, Ohio, and it was -5 outside. It was cold where I was. I had only $ 40.00 on me, I left all my credit cards and bank cards on the table and said to her, "Have a nice life". I was cold that night, and I had a big smile on my face. Like a 400- pound weight was off my shoulders. FREEDOM, FREEDOM, FREEDOM.

There are three kinds of lies

"Lies, damn lies, and statistics".

(Benjamin Disraeli) (1804---1881)

At the end of 2011, I started to be tired of being homeless, and I could see that God was trying to put that plan of His, moving in the right direction. So, I will need a job to restart my life, and go back to live in the society, and I know how it works, and why that sometime it doesn't work. Been there, done that. When you are homeless, it is very hard to keep a job. Too many obstacles in front of you. When you find a job, you have no food to eat at lunch time, you cannot take a shower to be ready for the next day, you have no spare clothing, and no money for transportation. These are the problems that we are facing when we did find a job, and trying to go forward. When the idea of getting out of homelessness was stronger for a couple of days straight, then I knew it was time to go, and I said to my God: You know what I am about to ask You, so here it is? I am tired to be homeless, so, I want You to find me a Job, I want also to be able to take a shower after work, I want a place to sleep, to have something to eat, and also to have spare clothing, so I can go to work the next day clean, and I am asking You all this in Jesus Name, Amen. After that was the beginning of the Thanksgiving prayers that I put into action, many times a day, and I continue to believe with all my heart that I already have that job. I was making some movies of 5 to 10 seconds long with my mind to help me seeing it better, that I already have that job.

Doing this many times a day, and continuing to believe day after day, and rejoicing when I was walking in the park where I was staying. Actually, I consider the entire USA to be my back yard. Six weeks passed, and one morning it was very windy and cold that November day, and I had to wait until 9:30 am before I could go into the library to keep myself warm. I was in the library for two hours when a man approached me and said; "Do you know me?" and I said, "Yes, you are Brian's brother." He said, do you want to work for me, for one week only, I said yes. He said you can stay at my home, take a shower after work, I will feed you, on the way home we will stop at the second-hand clothing store, so you can have a change of clothes, I probably said thank you, Father, for that new job, and all the trimming. One week passed, he paid me, and it was a Monday, he was ready to go to work, and I said to him, do you need me today, he said no, you can stay here though. I said no, I do not take advantage of someone, just drop me off to my spot, and when you will need me, you will know where I will be. So, I gave him $75.00 for the food and clothing, and he said no, I say yes. I do not take advantage of you, and he takes it. Every day, I was saying prayers of Thanksgiving for God to give him lots of work. Around one month later, one week before Christmas, he came to pick me up, and said to me, I have lots of work, do you want to come work for me. I was smiling when he told me about all the work he has now. This man does not believe in God, so what a relationship we did have. I did work for him 8 years on/off. When I became 65 years of age, I wasn't working much for the last 3 months, and I decided to go get my pension benefit. I figure it will take about 2 months before I get a check from them. Two days later, I received a check in my mailbox. I was stunned by how fast it was. Not, long after that my landlord sold the house where I was, and she pass a few months after that. I relocated to the other side of the town, and 2 ½ years later, I started to talk to God about what I want to do, and COVID-19 shows up, what a mess COVID did. I told God that I wants to write books, and that I want to get out of Las-Vegas, my body did not like the heat as much anymore. Three months later, I was back in Canada.

GOD IS GOOD ALL THE TIME, ALL THE TIME GOD IS GOOD

So, from 12 years old to today, I can see that God was preparing a plan that He had to change some time to time because of all the stupidity I did in my life. Today I am in "Daddy arms", and I am here to please Him.

"When you're going to tell the truth, you better make them laugh, otherwise they'll kill you"

George Bernard) (1856---1950)

Luke 10:25-28, Behold, a certain lawyer stood up and tested Him and said; Teacher, what shall I do to inherit Eternal Life? Jesus said to him; what is written in the Law? (The Law of Moses who is actually the Word of God, and it becomes the Law of Moses) Jesus answered and said; "You shall love the Lord your God with all your heart, with all your soul, with all your strength, and with all your mind. **Jesus never said; with all your mind,** He never ever said that. Look in Deuteronomy 6:5, you will see that God never ever said **with all your mind.** (That is another lie) It was added by these "freaking" bad theologians and bad scholars. **So, these words "with all your mind" should be erased from your Bible.** In Leviticus 19:18, God did say also; and love your neighbor as yourself. In verse 37 (Jesus was speaking to the lawyer), Jesus said, "Go and do likewise." Romans 10:9, Paul said; "When you confess with your mouth the Lord Jesus and believe in your heart that God has raise Him from the dead, you will be saved. It is not what the Law of Moses said. Moses said in his Law to believe with all your heart. You can see it is not the same; in your heart, compare to: **with all your heart.** Paul was not an Apostle of Jesus (As one of the 12), he was like you and me, a Disciple of Jesus, and God said that Paul was a **Chosen Vessel**. We have to be "Precise" when we speak. Many of the Apostles and Disciples, when they speak, they are not as "Precise" as they should be. We can see that; in your heart, compare to, with all your heart, that there is a big difference. When you believe in your heart in Jesus and God, and you are actually a religious person, because you are in religion, and you believe in your heart in Jesus and believe that you are a Christian (You might be close, only there is no cigars)

That word Christian it is a very tricky word in our language today. Religious Jews peoples, after the Resurrection of Jesus, started to kill all these Christians, they can find who did believed in Him. Since then, many other religions pops-up in the world, and every religion considers themselves to be a Christian. The first Christian was not actually a Christian they were a born-again Christian. Every born-again Denomination called themselves Christian, and they are wrong; they are not Christian: they are born-again Christian. We, born-again, know that the devil he is the father of all religions in this world, and religious peoples call themselves Christians.

When you put two and two together, you will find out that the devil has to be the most Christian of all. He is the father of them all religions, so, he has to be the most religious Christian of all Christians. This is why I am telling to all of you who are born-again, that you should say that you are a born-again Christian, and not a Christian. To all of you who are in a religion, you should rethink your own thinking. When you think about all these peoples who do not believe in God, and believe in the universe instead, where they do their "Shopping". These unbelievers, as we call them, they are actually are believers; **they believe and have Faith in their own words;** and that they will receive what they are asking. They are not born-again or religious, and they do not consider themselves Christian, for sure. They do not believe in their hearts; **they believe with all their heart.** To resume all this. Do not believe everything you read as the true Gospel. Be aloof. That the author is a Disciple or Apostle, still check it out first before you believe. (Because of all these bad theologians/scholars) Matthew 5:28, Jesus said: "Therefore, you shall be "Perfect" just as your Father in Heaven is "Perfect". This is what God does, "He believe with all His heart" when He believe---not in His heart, it is a no, no, to Him. Jesus said also: Do what My Father do, and you will be "Perfect" too. (Paraphrase) Matthew 7:21-23, Not everyone who says to Me, "Lord, Lord", will enter the Kingdom of Heaven. He is talking to the born-again people here, and not religious people. Only he who does the will of My Father in Heaven. Jesus, when He use the pronoun, he, Jesus is talking to our spirit when He said that, I will explain it later in the book, and there are millions of people who will not like to hear what I will be saying. (Especially the ladies) Many will say to Me, in that day, "Lord, Lord", have we not prophesied in Your Name, and cast out demons in Your Name, and do wonders in Your Name. We know that Jesus was speaking to the one who are born-again, and do not walk the walk, as God said in His Word. He is not speaking to religious people because they do not have Him as their "Personal Savior." There is no me, me, me, in Heaven say God. (This is reading between the lines) So, to the one who do not want to sing to Me, or open his/her mouth in church to worship Me, I say to you: "Thou shalt receive what you sow," and when there is no sowing, there will be no "harvest" either. This is why Jesus will say to you: "I do not know you". Outch, that one will hurt. It will be too late though; you cannot come back and redo it, too late is too late. I will repeat it again. Always be careful not to start believing right away, what you are hearing, and reading. (Check it out first) Apostles or not, or anyone else.

The bad theologians and scholars are the most painful pain in the butt, their fingers are all dirty, from the first Bible in the year 1200 to the year 1604 were very bad Bible, they were corrupt. It was not written by a plumber or an electrician either, it was written by Bad theologians and bad scholars, and they do not use "Precise" Words of God, even today. They are paraphrasing a lot, the way they see it, and the way to fit their own doctrine belief and religion. Be aloof. These bad theologians and bad scholars they really succeeded to; **PISS ME OFF,** and anyone who makes my Savior a liar. These bad theologians et bad scholars when they retouch a Bible, they cannot be trustworthy. In the four Gospels they make my Savior lying eight times, and it is impossible for Jesus to lie, except that he did eight times. As far as I am concern, theology is a trade that is seven time worst than a sinful prostitute. Now let's look at an example in 1 John 5:13, "Those things that I have written to you who believe in the name of the Son of God, that you may know that you have Eternal Life, and that you may continue to believe in the name of the Son of God." What do you see in that statement that you might think that Normand does not like at all? Is it the real words of John? We do not know that because we do not have the original writing for us to see. We know that bad theologians and bad scholars have dirty fingers (Have a religion in mind), and we know that religion and the devil do go hand in hand. So, why is it that John will say: "In the name of the Son of God", and on top of that, they don't even want to put a capital letter to the word Name, it smells of theology to me. Why is it, it did not say "In the Name of Jesus" here that smell again, it really smells bad. Sometimes when we are reading books in the Bible, we start to "Wonder", did the authors did write it like that? Jesus already said that every knee will bow to **THE NAME** of Jesus. The devil knows that, and he is not looking forward to that moment either, when he will have to bow to **THE NAME.** Not to Jesus, not to the Son of God, and not to God, only, to **THE NAME.** I do not believe John did made a mistake as huge as this one. When you are reading it with your eye glasses of religion, you will believe that believing in the Son of God will actually be your "ticket" to enter through the Gate of Heaven, without asking Jesus to come into your heart as your "Personal Savior", well, you are mistaking and dreaming. These bad theologians and bad scholars do not want you to see that it is in THE NAME the One Who did crush their religion to the ground. They do not like that at all, only, they will bow their knee to **THE NAME** of Jesus. It is the most "**POWERFUL NAME** of all names, **THE NAME** of Jesus, Amen, and Amen thank You Jesus that You sacrifice Yourself, and take my place on the tree, Thank You for that **Name---JESUS.**

"Half a truth is often a great lie"

(Benjamin Franklin) (1706---1790)

I will explain to you something, the way I am seeing different from how most of the religious and born-again people are seeing it. When these authors in the "New Covenant" are not precise when they speak, Satan saw that, and as the best lawyer that he is, and bringing doubts and lies, by the shovel like manure, he saw "Loop holes" in the authors when they are writing their Gospels, so, he is using these "Loop holes" to start a new religion, or many religions for the peoples to believe in his words. The clever way that he is using also, it is to change the words coming from the author's mouth, and put words that "Sound better" to the hearer, and people think that it is the real words of the author, when it is not. God want us to be precise or very specific when we speak His words, or when we are asking Him something. Our words are very important to Him; you can make sure of that. I will say be "**specifically precise**" when you are speaking to anyone, and be specially, precise when you are asking "DADDY" for something. These Apostles and Disciples they didn't have books as we have, and the Holy Spirit has to teach them quite a bit about Jesus, God, as far as the future (Rapture, and the first Resurrection) and to watch out because the enemy is watching our steps, and hear our own words, so, we have to be aware of that, because we might become a victim of their wrong doings---be very aware of that. I am not saying that what John said in these verses that he was wrong. I am saying that he didn't have all the information that we born-again has today. Were they the words of the bad theologians, and bad scholars, who did rewrite it the way they wanted to us to read it, and make us think that it was the author words. (The 66 books in the condensed Bible) Matthew 18:2-3, As far as Faith is concerned, Jesus called a little child to Him, set him in the midst of them, and said: "Assuredly, I say to you, unless you are converted and become as a little child, you will by no means enter the Kingdom of Heaven." One thing about little children is that they believe (Almost) everything we tell them, because they are using their Faith all the time. It is why that God wanted you to become as little children, because He wants you to have as much Faith as they have. Especially when you are a new "Baby" in Faith, and He wants you to use it that Faith as often as you can. Tell two 5-year-old child to go in the living room to see that new puppy, and they will run as fast as they can to see that new puppy. Because they already believe that it is the truth (They probably see it in their mind as they were running).

Only it was a "joke" from Uncle Jack. Actually, it was not a joke, it was a lie disguised as a joke. We have to see it and speak it as it is—a lie. What about "Santa" or the "tooth fairy" do they believe in them, too? I will say, yes, they do believe and with all their heart. When they will become pre-teen, they will not use their Faith as much as when they were little children. When they will become an adult, they will not use it much anymore like they were as a little child. Sometimes when you speak a lie, you say to the hearer, it was only a "White lie." Why is it a white lie anyway; should it be a "dark lie," because it came from the one who is living in the pit? (Darkness) Tell the truth, parents, and do not tell them that Santa exists, because as smart as they are, living in a small apartment where this is no chimney, they will ask, "How, can Santa come since we do not have a chimney. As a parent, you will probably answer it with another lie. What about the half cookie, and half glass of milk, and you will say to your child, "Look", Santa came and drank some of the milk and took a bite of the cookie. That's another lie, and will continue to be compounded until he/she is old enough and hear some stories in the school yard. When you want your child to be truthful, should it start at home with the parents; the grandparents are as bad, too? Look at the similarity between **Santa** and **Satan**---a lie is a lie---period.

"We are not retreating;

We are advancing in

Another direction"

(Douglas Macarthur) (1880—1964)

Philippians 4:19, Paul said: "My God shall supply all your need according to His riches in Glory by Christ Jesus. So, we should be in abundance since all those years that we ask in the Name of Jesus. His Words say so, only when we will act on it. You already know that it will not happen overnight, or right after you say a couple of Thanksgiving prayers. You have to continually declare what God's Words say; up to went the "Words" will get into your spirit, and will be a "Part of you" always, that is, when you will continue to declare it. The Words of God will get you out of poverty or any situations unpleasant in your life.

It will give you a healthy body, and much more, it will always be "According to your Faith", when you will believe with all your heart. When you did accept Jesus as your "Personal Savior" and believe with all your heart, and that He died for you, **AT THAT INSTANT,** you become automatically Righteous and automatically Blessed. 2 Peter 1:4, By which you have been given to us exceedingly great and precious Promises, that through these you may be partakers of the Divine Nature. What is the Divine Nature of God? The answer is Righteousness, and we are partakers of the Righteousness of God. 2 Corinthians 5:21, For He made Him Who knew no sin to be sin for us, that we might become Righteousness; of God in Him. Charles Capps quote: Your head didn't get saved, your body didn't get saved, your spirit was born-again. You were created in the Righteousness of God through Christ Jesus, with God on the inside. James 3:1, My brothers/sisters, let not many of you become teachers, knowing that we will receive a stricter judgment.

Be careful what's coming out of your mouth.

When you speak in the world, do not speak like the world; especially when you don't pay attention to what's coming out of your mouth. The people in your congregation will speak what they heard from the pulpit. God did say that my people (Children) are destroyed by "Lack of knowledge". That teacher (Preacher)will be judged more strictly by his/her own words, who will judge him/her, and what you think will happen to all these theologians and scholars who are teaching us. Outch again and again. Everything you did as a teacher will go through the furnace, and when it will come out, that will be your reward. Gold or a pile of ashes? When they will receive ashes, they still go to Heaven, some of them; because it will happen in Heaven, only, the reward will not be the same as you heard it will be. So, I will urge you, teachers, and even you preachers to be very careful about what you say and how you say it. Because your own words will judge you. Do you know what the Knowledge of God is? Let's go to Proverbs that some are the Wisdom of God. Proverb 1:7, The fear of the Lord is the beginning of Knowledge. Proverb2:1-9, My child, when you receive My Words, and treasure My command within you, and that you incline your ear to My Wisdom, and apply your heart to Understanding; Yes, when you cry out for discernment, and lift up your voice to Understanding, when you seek Her as silver, and seek for Her as a "Hidden treasure" then; you will understand the fear of the Lord, and the Knowledge of God. For the Lord gives Wisdom; from His mouth comes Knowledge and Understanding; He stores up "Sound Wisdom" for the upright; He is a shield to those who walk Uprightly; He guards the path of justice, and preserves the way of His saints. (You) Then you will understand Righteousness and justice, equity and every good path. Proverb 9:10, The fear of the Lord is the beginning of Wisdom, and the Knowledge of the Holy One is Understanding. Proverb 4:7-9, Wisdom is the principal thing; therefore, get Wisdom and in all your getting, get Understanding. Exalt Her, and She will promote you; She will bring you honor when you embrace Her. She will place on your head an ornament of Grace; a crown of Glory she will deliver to you. Proverb 8:14, Counsel is Mine and sound Wisdom; I am Understanding, I have Strength. Proverb 7:4-5, Say to Wisdom, "You are my sister", and call Understanding your nearest kin. That they may keep you from the immoral woman (Religion), from the seductress who flatters with her words. Revelation 17:5, On her forehead a name was written:

MYSTERY, BABYLON THE GREAT, THE MOTHER OF HARLOTS AND

ABOMINATIONS OF THE EARTH.

Proverb 5:1-6, My child, pay attention to My Wisdom; lend your ear to My Understanding, that you may preserve discretion, and your lips may keep Knowledge. For the lips of an immoral woman (Religion) drip honey, and her mouth is smoother than oil; and in the end she is bitter than wormwood, sharper as a two-edged sword. Satan words (Religion) are sharp as two edges, a sword (Be aloof). Hebrews 4:12, Paul said, "For the Word of God is living and powerful, and sharper than any two-edged sword, piercing even to the division of soul and spirit, and of joints and marrow, and is a discerner of the thoughts and intents of the heart. (God's sword is quite a bit much sharper than Satan sword) 2 Corinthians 4:3-4, Paul said, "Even when our Gospel is veiled (Hard to see), it is veiled to those who are perishing, whose minds the god of this age has blinded, who do not believe, lest the Light of the Gospel of the Glory of Christ, Who is the image of God, should shine on them.

"A lie as speed, except,

truth has endurance".

(Edgar J. Mohn)

Did you ever wonder about the virgin birth? There are lots of people who have a hard time to try to comprehend that it is a Miracle. I am not one of them (The doubters) because I know that it is impossible for God to lie. There are some theologians and scholars, and religious people, who still do not believe it, that it is a Miracle. The Word of God are Word of Truth, there is no deceitfulness in them, there is no doubts in them either, so every Word of God is our True Word. God always speaks first; His Words and His Power make it happen. Hebrews 1:3, Who being the Brightness of His Glory, and the express image of His Person, and upholding all things by the Word of His Power. The Holy Spirit was teaching Paul in his spirit, and put it the way that God wanted us to see it, and read it also. The Holy Spirit didn't say the Power of His Word; He said by the Word of His Power. We know that in His Word that there is Power in it, only, not all His Power is in it. Some of His Power are in it, and not all of His Power is in it. This is how the Holy Spirit wants Paul to see it, that it is the right way to speak it. Mark 11:22, Jesus said: "Have Faith in God", and it is not how God says it. (Another lie) In many Bibles today, you will read it this way, "Have Faith in God". In the year that the Authorized King James Bible came out (1611), it was written "Have the Faith **of** God". These bad theologians and bad scholars they did it again, changing God's Word for their own words, and also to go along with their own doctrine. It is not the same meaning. In 1769 they rewrite it from the 1611 Bible. Have Faith in God and Have the Faith **of** God. It is two different meanings. So, they want us to speak their words, instead of speaking the Word of God. When you have Faith in God, it means that you do not need to be involved, you do not have to believe with all your heart, you just let Him handle it. When you read have the Faith **of** God, it means that God wants you to be involved with Him, and wants you to start to believe with all your heart. He wants you to use the same kind of Faith that He is using. In a way, you do "Imitate" your Father, and it is a flattering to Him to see that. When you have Faith in God, you do not "Imitate" Him. These bad theologians and bad scholars they did it on purpose because they do not want you to read, and speak the Word of God. They want us to read and speak their words according to their doctrine dictates. They are all dead today, and the devil is already training some new ones to replace them. The new one will most likely will continue to do more damage. **They really piss me off.** Before and after 1611, these yack-ass we're replaced by other ones just like them. The problem is that all the damage they did, they did it on purpose, and they, (The damages) are there to stay. It is there for us to see it, and make us believe that it is actually the Word of God. The leaders of all Denominations they do not like to care much about all these "Purpose words putting on purpose" that these religious theologians and scholars did to all the Bible out there. These leaders will rewrite another Bible and are using the same "rotten words" that they put in the first Bible. This will continue up to when someone will decide to do something about that. (And it will be me, granted --- I believe it). I will repeat what Charles Capps said: Your head didn't get saved, your body didn't get saved, only your spirit was born-again. You were created in the Righteousness of God through Christ Jesus, with God on the inside. (Your heart) When you will receive that new spirit in you, it will not affect your whole body, your heart only. It is not supposed to be about ourself, it is all about Him-- not you. You cannot let the "old you" to take charge in your life. I can tell you that your body does not always want to do the same things that your spirit would like to do. You will have to take charge of your body, and not the body to take charge of your spirit.

"How is the world ruled and led to war?

Diplomats lie to journalists and believe these lies;

when they see them in print"

(Karl Kraus) (1874 --- 1936)

James 1:21, Therefore lay aside all filthiness, and overflow of wickedness, and receive with meekness the implanted Word, which is able to save your soul. In the 1611 Authorized King James Bible, the word is "Engrafted," not implanted. In today's Bible, they are using most of them the word implanted instead. Why change it when that word engrafted was fine? Engrafted to me means having the Word of God "Tattooed" in your heart, So, it is there to stay with you always. It is actually the Word of God that you can carry with you at all times. Do not listen to or have a conversation with the voice in your head; it is not the voice of God. When God speaks to you, He will speak in your heart, not in your intellect. (Mind) The enemy will speak in your mind, he cannot change your heart, his job is to make you to do it, he wants you to change your mind so that you and only you will go and change your heart. The voice in your head is an idiot, and when you have a conversation with an idiot, and you both agree, will you say that you are becoming an idiot also? Have the Word of God "Engrafted" in your heart. God, when He speaks to us, it is in our hearts. God will not hang around in our mind when He knows that there is an idiot in there. When you pray or ask a request to God, make sure you do not have any doubts in you; and coming out of your mouth also. Start to pay attention to your own words when you speak; you have ears, well, use them then. When you are listening to your words, and hear the word "IF", it is a no, no, don't; a "IF" is a doubt. I am betting that you didn't know that, only now you realize that you didn't pay attention before at all to this, and now you know this is why you didn't receive what you are asking for. When you pray or you are talking to God, and have a doubt, or doubts, I am telling you this is why you do not receive. When you will continue to do it the same way as before, you will continue to not receive, how can you expect to receive? Change demands patience, strength. When laziness is involved in your body, you will go nowhere with laziness. Change demand "Effort". It is not your body who is in charge of your spirit; it is your spirit who should be in charge. Because laziness thinking is: The less I do, the less I want to do." God did say to be precise when you speak, not just to Him, to anyone also be precise, so, when it is time to talk to Him, you will be precise, because this is what you do always---be a precise talker. When you are using doubt words, that it is your enemy words, and you believe with all your heart, what you are saying, God says: "Thou shalt receive according to your mouth" (I paraphrase). That you speak God's Words, and believe them, thou shalt receive. When you speak the devil's words and believe them, thou shalt receive what you believe. When you speak to God, He is listening to your words, and at the same time He is reading your heart to see what in it, and when He sees that you believe only to a certain degree, He will not give it to you. He will say that this Child of Mine does not believe with all his/her heart. Can you see now why it is very important to have the Word of God "Tattooed" in your heart, for the simple reason that there are no "doubts" in God's Word. Pay attention to what's coming out of your mouth---period. Also, pay attention to someone else words; and especially their actions. When someone is speaking, listen carefully to the words he/she is using, and especially watch their actions. Listen to that beautiful "fictional" story that I put together for you. Let's say there a man speaking to a big room full of enthusiastic people, and anxious to hear him of what he has to say. He will touch on many issues for two hours straight. So, lifting his hand high, he said; lift your hand when someone is pregnant in this room? He counted how many hands were up. Asking another question, he lifted his hand again, and asked how many who are child's molesters are in the room? Again, lifting his hand, he asked how many people have venereal disease? Lifting his hand again, he asked how many of you are cheating on their spouse? When the two hours are over, almost everyone is clapping and saying how good he was as a speaker. It happens that I was in the room also. I was standing waiting to go out when a few people who knew me approached me. One of them said to me, wow, what a speaker, I really love that speaker, what do you think, Normand? This guy did ask me a precise question, and I will give him a precise answer. It is because you are an idiot; what, why do you say; that I am an idiot? I said to him, did you pay attention to his own actions when he was speaking to us. No, not really, why? Every time when he was asking us a question, he lifted his hand. Can you see that this man does not pay attention to his own words? Why should I believe his own words when he himself doesn't even believe his own words? How come you know all this? I read that in a book, and the author was explaining this to us, the readers. Can you see that the speaker lifted his hand always? He is cheating on his spouse, have a venereal disease, he is a child molester, and to top off that he is pregnant. That was a heck of a story. When a 72-year-old lady who was speaking to a room full of women about health issues, and said, lift your hand the one who is with child, and she left her hand. What will you do? Do you think that this speaker believed what she is doing? I don't think so. She doesn't pay attention to her own words; why should I believe her. You can ask some kids in the backyard, who want to go to the circus with me today, lift your hand. I can tell you they do not need you to raise your hand to show them how it works; they already know it. The thing with us adult it seems that we the adult have to show another adult how to do it. **Put this in your pipe and smoke it.**

"Repetitions do not transform

a lie into a truth"

(Franklin Roosevelt) (1882-1945)

The devil wants your mouth.

The devil does not want us to learn that we have the Power with our words to "Bind things, and loose things" on the earth with our own words. The devil wants us to give him control of our mouths, so that we will speak his words, and that he can wreak havoc on us. The devil wants your mouth, plain and simple. God created man in His own image, and He is Truthful, and every word of God are Word of Truth. angels of Light do not have the ability to use their own words, the angels of darkness, it is another story, though, they can. God is everywhere; Satan he is not he can only be in one place at the time. God did say that evil is everywhere, and Satan can only be at one place. It is not because that Satan is evil that he is everywhere. Evil is, only, not Satan. So, now we can see that Satan has to ask his demon of darkness to do his dirty work, so that it appears that he is everywhere, and we should not assume that. He wants us to learn to speak words of fear, hatred, division, selfishness, confusion, unforgiveness, and jealousy (Jealous of a person beauty, or a gift that someone received at birth). God did say that He is a jealous God, because He doesn't want for us to worship another god created by us. He doesn't want us to worship a human being as a god, and He doesn't want us to think, me, me, me, about ourselves. It should be all about Him, and Him only, no other gods. God hate—sin, only He loves the sinner, we are all sinners, except we are not sinning at all times, some do, and they do not care because God does not exist---to them. It is our action(s) that God hates, and not us that He hates. Hatred becomes a sin when you hate your neighbor as yourself. So, God is a hater of sin and sins only. The devil will always go 180 degrees from what God says. The devil wants you to hate everything and everyone, it is easier. He wants us to put everything and everyone in the same basket, and hate what it is inside that basket. You can hate your car, your job, that ok. I t became a sin when you hate another Human being. The devil wants you to hate your neighbor, the voice in your head says so. Hate that person, they think they are better than us, go ahead, hate your neighbor. Only that voice in your head will never finish that phrase of God that says. Thou shalt not hate your neighbor "As yourself." That voice will tell you to hate your neighbor, only he will never say the whole thing. Because even when you are in a religion, you still are a good person as long as you do good things. When you will hear to hate that person like you hate yourself, this is when you will draw the line, and say: What as myself? When your words agree with the Word of God, you are actually thwarting the devil's plan. God is his enemy, and he doesn't like it when you are saying God's Words. We, as a living being we have choices, and the devil wants you to choose him, give me your mouth, and that choice is yours; it is a no, no, to

God, for us to speak like our enemy speaks. Here are some of the Wisdom Proverbs that we should read sometimes to fortify us. **PROVERBS. 4:24,** Put away from you a deceitful mouth, and put perverse lips far from you. **6:2,** My Child, when you become surety for your friend, when you have shaken hands in pledge for a stranger, you are snared by the words of your mouth; you are taken by the words of your mouth. **6:12,** A worthless person, a wicked man/woman, walks with a perverse mouth. **8:7-8,** (Wisdom says) For My mouth will speak truth; wickedness is an abomination to My lips. All the Words of My mouth are with Righteousness; nothing crooked or perverse is in them. **8:13,** The fear of the Lord is to hate evil; and arrogance and the evil way, and the perverse mouth I hate. **10:11,** The mouth of the Righteous is a well of life, and violence covers the mouth of the wicked. **10:31-32,** The mouth of the Righteous brings forth Wisdom, and the perverse tongue will be cut out. The lips of the Righteous know what is acceptable, and the mouth of the wicked what is perverse. **12:14,** A man/woman will be satisfied with good by the fruit of his/her mouth, and the recompense of a man's/woman's hands will be rendered to him/her. **13:3,** He/she who guards his/her mouth preserves his/her life, and he/she who opens wide his/her lips shall have destruction. **14:3,** In the mouth of a fool is a rod of pride, and the lips of the wise will preserve them. **15:2,** The tongue of the wise uses; knowledge rightly, and the mouth of fools pours forth foolishness. **15:4,** A wholesome tongue is a tree of life, and perverseness in it breaks the spirit. **17:20,** He/she who has a deceitful heart finds no good, and he/she who has a perverse tongue falls into evil. **18:21,** Death and life are in the power of the tongue, and those who love it will eat its fruit. **21:23,** Whoever guards his/her mouth and tongue keeps his/her soul from troubles. **3:5,** Trust in the Lord with all your heart, and lean not on your own understanding; in all your ways acknowledge Him, and He shall direct your paths.

"What is the truth, that

a lie agreed upon"?

(Friedrick Nietzsche) (1844-1900)

A human being has a human body. So, we are a being (A spirit) and that being has a soul, and a body, and that body as a mind. Genesis 1:26, Then God said; Let Us make man in Our image, according to Our likeness. (God is 3 in 1, He is a triune) So, we have a body, mind, and soul. (A spirit) Our body is visible; we already know that because we can see each other, and your body is mortal, we can thank Adam /Eve for that. The parts that are invisible in your body is your emotions and your thoughts, and they are also mortal. Your soul is invisible. In your soul, you have your conscience, and also your intention. (For decision-making) Your spirit will live with God or with Satan on Eternity on Eternity. You are the only one who are doing the choosing, and where you want to be. The choice will not be made after death; it is before death. Choose wisely because too late is too late. You choose the Almighty God when accepting Jesus as your "Personal Savior" in your heart, or you choose a religion or no religion at all, and follow the one (Satan) who wants to be the god himself. I am preparing you to tell you that you will be stunned from my words in a few pages. Don't be mad yet; keep your strength for later. I will say that a million over a million will not like to hear what I am saying. Especially women and young ladies, except it has to be said; and need to be heard out loud. Maybe the hurt will be in your heart. I know that it will be a **shock** when you will hear it. You might put that book aside for a while, you will not like to hear that **Big Nugget** of information coming to you. Exodus 3:14, God says to Moses; I am **THAT** I am. In the Authorize King James it said: I am that I am. In the New King James version, it said: I am Who I am? These bad theologians and bad scholars they did it again, changing a word for another. They change the word "That' for "Who", and it is wrong. When you are reading, I am Who I am, it doesn't mean that His Name is "I am." In another Bible, it reads; "It is what it is" that doesn't give us His Name. In some other Bible, it said: I will become what I choose to become. (In the future) In another one, it said: I am what I am it doesn't say what His Name is. In another one, it said: I will be what I will be? (Is it a question mark) These bad theologians and bad scholars they really piss me off. They are in all the Denominations and in all religions, and look at all the damages they do on our planet. They do not agree much which each other except that they all agreed in one, and only one thing. That Jesus was from the planet Earth, and was not a Klingon or a Volcan. (Volcan are known for their logic) God said: "I am That I am" what it means is: "I am The I am?" John 10:34, Jesus saying; "Is it not written in your Law" (Moses Law) I Said: "You are gods"? (Elohim's ps:82.6) So, God Himself call us gods (elohim's) He is The Elohim among Elohim's. I want you to think when the Gentiles had many different gods in whatever religion they had.

These gods were nothing with no power whatsoever. This is why He said that; "I am That I am." not an idol made of wood, silver, gold, or stone. So, God He is actually saying; I am above all gods on this earth; "I am **The I am.**" Although acknowledging Him that He exist is not enough for you to receive your "Ticket" to go to Heaven, even when your religion says so. God is Elohim, idols are elohim's according to men, men/women are elohim's, and this is why God said in Psalm 82 because He wants us to be just like Him---minus the capital letter and His power (Of course).

"A lie is more comfortable than doubt, more useful than love, more lasting than truth"

(Gabriel Garcia) (1927-2014)

Exodus 7:1, God said to Moses: See, I have made you God to Pharaoh, and Aaron your brother shall be a Prophet. Genesis 3:4-5, Then the serpent said to the woman: You will surely not die. (Satan knew that we will die **Spiritually,** and that your spirit will live forever, so it was a ½ truth and 1 lie) For God knows in the day you eat of it your eyes will be opened (1 truth), and you shall be as gods (Satan didn't know that far, away in the future that God will say is Psalm 82.6 **You are gods**. So, it was a 1 lie again, knowing good and evil. (1 truth) So, he said 2 1/2 lies and 2 truths. God wants us to be just like Him. This is why God said that He is the **Elohim among elohim's**, He wants us to be just like Him. He really wants us to follow after His own steps. 1 John 2:5-6, Whoever keeps His Word, truly the Love of God is Perfected in him/her, by this we know that we are in Him. He/she who says he/she abides in Him ought himself/herself also to walk just as He walked. 1 John 2-3, Beloved, now we are Children of God; and it has not been revealed, what we shall be, and we know that when He is revealed, we shall be like Him, for we shall see Him as He is, and everyone who has this believe in Him purifies himself/herself, just as He is pure. Matthew 5:48, Therefore you shall be Perfect, just as your Father in Heaven is Perfect. Luke 6:46, Why do you call Me Lord, Lord, and not do the things I say? Ephesians 5:1, Therefore be imitators of God as dear children. (With your Faith) God wants us to think like Him, talk like Him, act like Him, pray like Him, have Faith like Him, and certainly walk like Him.

I will tell you the **Big Nugget** now, and what I said to Him in 2017. When you read God's Words, Wisdom Words in Proverbs, or when Jesus said something, I find out that they **almost always** are using the article **He** not she when they talk to us. They God, Jesus, Wisdom are not using the articles her, she, woman, and daughter; it is always him, he, son, man. So, I ask God and say to Him: **Are you sexist Father** I am not saying that you are, it just that it looks like it? I think Father that when I will make the trip to see You in Heaven, that I will ask the "JUDGES" of the universe, that I am thinking of bringing You to court, and I will ask You: "Are You sexist?" I will bring Your own Words, the Words of Wisdom, of God and the Words of Jesus also, because Jesus said: **Every Words I speak are the Words of My Father.** I will not bring the Words that You said from the **Old Covenant**, only the one in the **New Covenant**, the Words that Jesus came to Teach. After the Resurrection, Jesus said to John in, Revelation 2:7 **He** who has an ear let **Him** hear what the Spirit says to the churches. To **Him** who overcomes I will give to eat from the tree of life, which is in the midst of the Paradise of God. Revelation 2:11, **He** who has an ear, let **Him** hear what the Spirit says to the churches. **He** who overcomes shall not be hurt by the second death. Revelation 2:17, **He** who has an ear, let **Him** hear what the Spirit says to the churches. To **Him** who overcomes I will give some of the hidden manna to eat. I will give **Him** a white stone, and on the stone a new name written which no one knows except **Him** who receives it. Revelation 2:26-28, **He** who overcomes and keeps My Works until the end, to **Him** I will give power over the nations **He** shall rule them with a rod of iron; they shall be dashed to pieces like the potter's vessels, as I also received from My Father; and I will give **Him** the Morning Star. Revelation 3:5, **He** who overcomes shall be clothed in white garments, and I will not blot out **His** name from the BOOK OF LIFE; and I will confess **His** name before My Father, and before His angels. Revelation 3:12, **He** who overcomes, I will make **Him** a pillar in the Temple of My God, and **He** shall go out no more. I will write on **him** the Name of My God, and the name of the city of My God, the NEW JERUSALEM, which comes out down out of Heaven from My God. I will write on **Him,** My new Name. Revelation 3:21, To **Him** who overcomes I will grant to sit with me on My Throne, as I also overcame and sat down with My Father on His Throne. Revelation 22:7, Behold, I am coming quickly! Blessed is **He** who keeps the Words of the prophecy of this Book. Revelation 22:11, **He** who is unjust, let **Him** be unjust still; **He** who is filthy, let **him** be filthy still; **he** who is Righteous, let **him** be Righteous still, **He** who is Holy, let **him** be Holy still. Ephesians 1:5, Paul receiving Teaching and guidance from the Holy Spirit said, "Having predestined us to adoption as sons by Jesus Christ to Himself."

This is what I will say to the JUDGES of the universe, this is God's Words, and nobody else. I will finish my testimony, and I will say to God: Tomorrow it is Your turn to speak. In all these Words of God, I didn't see any articles, her, she, woman, and daughter, I know for a fact that since the DAY OF PENTECOST to today era, that they had to have been million, over million of women, and young ladies who did accept Jesus has their Personal Savior in their heart. I was feeling pretty certain that I would win my case against God, that it does appear that He is sexist, I did not say that He was. So, two hours later I said to God: Your case doesn't look good right now, and You know what, it is very hard for me to believe that You are guilty. It can pass my mind that You are guilty, unless there is something that You know, and do not want to tell us, the **why** You are using only the article he and not she. I said to God: I want You to tell me what it is Father, what You are hidden from us. It is very hard for me to believe that You made a mistake as huge as this one. So, Father tells me. I am asking You to tell me **why** and I know that it is impossible for You to make a mistake, so I know that there is something there, and I just cannot see it. So, I am asking You to give me this information that You are hiding from us, and I am asking You this in Jesus Name. Thank You, thank You, Father. That night when I was in bed, I was saying Thanksgiving prayers, because I really believe that I did receive that answer by Faith, and I finally fall as sleep. Everything what I told you is the absolute true.

"I never give them hell. I just told the truth, and they thought it was hell"

(Harry Truman) (1884- 1972)

So, the next day I wasn't working, and I was watching tv, and a commercial came, and like I always do, I grab the remote, and put the tv on mute. As I was looking at the screen I heard in my heart, the answer, the famous answer I was looking for **why**. When I heard it, I was stunned, I think I closed the TV. So, when I heard It, I say to God, wow; You just win Your case. This is what I heard: **It's because that there is no female spirit, they are all male spirits. I was stunned**. I start to think about the fourth dimension where the Spirits live. God, Jesus, Holy Spirit, angels of Light, and the **pit** where the angels of darkness live, all of these spirits are male spirits, the only female Spirit in the entire universe is Wisdom. (Wisdom of God)

I will like to talk to you about Her, it's just that it is a two-hour teaching. Lots of women and young ladies, when they will hear this, they will be in **shock**, and probably will start to call me names, that's ok ladies, I will take the abuse. Is it what Jesus said that people will do to you as they did to Me. I was wondering **why** that God did create the universe with male spirits only, except Wisdom. I remember a saying that people said sometime, to someone. When you see someone doing business in a way that you do not like, and you will go and talk to the owner of the business, and tell the owner, I do not like the way you are running your business, the owner of the business will most likely say to you; this is my business, and I do it the way I see fit, and when you do not like it, go ahead and start your own business. This is what that God might say to us, when we tell Him; I do not like it the way it is, only male spirits **except Wisdom**, I do not like it, and God will say; start your own universe then, and do it the way you want it. You probably will say, I cannot do that, and God will say to you; **I KNOW.** Matthew 22:23-30, The same day the Sadducees, who say that there is no Resurrection, came to Him and ask Him, saying; Teacher, Moses said that when a man died, having no children, his brother should marry his wife, and raise up offspring for his brother. Now there were with us seven brothers. The first died after he had married, and having no offspring, left his wife to his brother. Like wise the second also, and the third, even to the seventh. Last of all, the woman died also. Therefore, in the Resurrection, whose wife of all seven will she be, for they all had her? Jesus answered and said to them; you are mistaken, not knowing the Scriptures nor the Power of God. For in the Resurrection, they neither marry nor are given in marriage, and are like angels in Heaven, angels of Light are called **sons of God**, not **daughters of God.** Matthew 22:30, For in the Resurrection they neither marry nor are given in marriage, only, they are like angels of God in Heaven. I will tell you something I do not like it either, who am I to contradict my God creation. That's His business and He is doing it the way He wanted to be. Genesis 1:11, **according to its own kind**, God has a soul, a mind, and His Spirit is a male. Now we can understand it better now, that all the spirits in this earth have, a soul, a mind, and a body, our different gender as nothing to do for us to create a spirit, we human we can create male and female body only, not the spirit. We might not like it only, we have to live with the idea, that we are all male spirits. Did you remember that I told you that the real you are that invisible spirit, and **he** is also a god **Elohim** on this earth. Jesus, He is the Lord of lords. Jesus never said that He is the King of kings and queens.

39

He never said that He is the Lord of lords and ladies. So, when you will put 1+1 together you will see that you are a male spirit who is a god, a king, and a lord on this earth. It is hard to digest these information's, only we know that 1+1=Truth. We have to think now that when we will be in His Kingdom for 1000 years, we will be all male spirits. When we die on this earth, our spirit will leave the body, and we will not remember that, and what gender we have, because when the spirit is out of your body, your memories, your hopes, your gender, your brain, all of these will stay with the body. We cannot bring our brain with us because of the blood in it. Our blood is contaminated by Adam's falls it is not our flesh that is the problem it is our blood. Our blood is polluted, and it is the Truth, even when we don't like it.

"It takes two to speak the truth,

one to speak and another to hear"

(Henry David) (1817-1862)

When preachers tell us that every person born on this earth since Cain are sinner because of our flesh, it is a freaking lie, it's not true. Because Jesus has to be a sinner also. When a woman is with child, the scientists discovered that the woman does not supply her blood to the baby; it is the man who supplies it. Jesus did not have a human Father, and Mary did not supply that blood either, it was the Faith of Mary in her heart, and she started to believe, and said to the angel, **"Let it be according to your Word".** She started to believe with all her heart that she will have the Son of God. The Holy Spirit came when she was sleeping and covered her, and implanted the "Seed" That God said in Genesis 3:15, "And I will put enmity between you (Satan) and the woman, and between your seed (us) and her Seed (Jesus), that is the second head of the Trinity, that is the Son of God. The Holy Spirit did put that Seed Who is the Word, in her egg, and the Word became flesh. Do not think that it was the sperm of God, it wasn't so. It was the "Word" Who became flesh for us. Now are you ready for another "Big Nugget". Everybody on this earth is male spirit, even Mary, the mother of Jesus. She did have a **he** spirits, like any-other-one on this earth. God created the universe the way He wanted to be. He created the earth with male, and female in it, so, that they

40

can procreate. Do not forget that our body is only a "temporary housing" for our spirit, when "**he**" is on this earth. It will take some time for the people in this world to comprehend this, and let go the "old adage". This I do believe that it will be hard to digest all of this. Specially the Catholic church, they will not be please, I can tell you that for a fact. (ask me--- do I care about that) Every religion and Denomination might be mad at me, it's ok, I can live with that, it is not about me, never will be, it is about the Truth, and God say that the Truth shall make you free, thank You, Father. You know, when I say earlier for you to not believe what's coming out of someone's breath, or what you are reading. Specially when it is the first time that you are hearing it, or are reading it. One of the things I am telling you is for you to not believe it right away, even what I might say makes sense, I will say to you -- don't. The second thing for you to do is to do your "homework", check it out, and see is it True. Go and check in your Bible, and we know that these Bibles of ours are not the most accurate books out there, only, we do not have choices, it's the only one we got. (For right now) Check all these chapters and verses that I did mention, you have a Bible, then check it out yourselves, do not be lazy, check it out. When everything is to your "satisfactory" then and only, then you can start to believe. It is not my words in these books; they are the Words of God. This is when these bad theologians they did not change the Word of God for their own words. In these Bibles, you will never find the words of Normand in it, I wasn't there, I was born in 1954. There is a lot of information to digest right now. Read it again, slowly, and ask the Holy Spirit Who is your Guide and Teacher, to give you Light on your recherche. When you do not ask, how can you receive? Only when you ask. Jesus was a human being Who came from a human being, His mother. His mother was a sinner as far as God is concern, because she came in this world from her biologically father, whose blood was polluted because of the fall of Adam. Jesus, blood was Holy from the start of Him becoming an embryo and a human being. Even His brothers didn't want to follow "THE WAY" that Jesus was Teaching, His sisters I do not know. They were still believing in their religion as the way to go to Heaven. We know now that later, after the Resurrection that some (Or all) changed their mind, and saw the writing on the wall, so to speak. It is not because they have the same mother, that they will become a **"Child of God"**, even Mary His Mother will have to pray the Father in Heaven, and ask Jesus to become her "Personal Savior." Anyone on this route will have to do it the same way, and believe with all their heart, and then you will become the "Child of God" (No favorite). So, when Jesus spoke in the "New Covenant" and He is using the articles "**he**" and "him", and when He was Teaching after the Resurrection, He was still using these articles "he" and "**him**". We can see by now that the "he" and "**him,**" that He was speaking to our spirit. Every Words of Jesus were the Words of God, speaking with the mouth of Jesus that the witnesses heard, and not His own Words. It is impossible for God to lie so, Jesus as to tell the true the whole time He was speaking. Will some of you will rethink your original thinking when you hear people say," I can't wait to see my grandmother, my mother, or my son, my daughter, my sister, my brother, my spouse when I will be in Heaven. Because this is what we heard by these born-again Christian for the last 500 years at least (It will not surprise me) that you will be together on Eternity on Eternity. Well, now you just realize that what I say it is hurting your heart at the moment. You cannot forget that, we will all be change, your own you will not look the same way as before, you can make sure of that. Your skin color will not be the same as here on earth. When you are a short-statured person or a very tall person, it is not what you will be. You are a heavy person, you will not be the same person, and nobody will remember anyone. Your intellect, and even your religious leaders, will tell you that I am a liar---go and check it out. Recherche it, and check it out, and do not believe right from the bat what I say, recherche it, now the ball is in your court, it is up to you to believe or not believe. It is you who will decide who to follow, what God is saying, or what doctrine that men did invent for you to believe. I will tell you that I know human, and when laziness started to take control of your body, your "doom" as far I am concern, unless you decide to change.

"Lying to ourselves is more deeply ingrained than lying to others"

(Fyodor) (1821-1881)

Look and hear what preachers from all Denominations said when a born-again died, that you will be with Jesus instantly. It is not scriptural, and none the less they continue to lie to their congregation. Lot of people follow their preacher blindly, and when he will tell them something that they want to hear, they will stay. $$$$$$$$$$$$$$$ is everything, for the leaders of any Denomination churches----- yeah. I will like to thank Andy Burnett and Erik Jones; two preachers who do preach as God say it. Listen to these verses about when you will die, where you will go.

Dead people "sleep' in unconsciousness, they don't think and feel anything. Job 14:12, So, man lies down and does not rise. Till the Heavens are no more, they will not awake nor be roused from their sleep. Daniel 12:2, Many of those who sleep in the dust of the earth shall awake, some to the everlasting life, some to shame and everlasting contempt. John 11:11, "Our friend Lazarus sleep; however, I will go that I may wake him up." Then His Apostles said; "Lord, he sleeps, he will get well." However, Jesus; spoke of his death, though they thought that He was speaking about taking rest in a sleep. Then Jesus said to them plainly; "Lazarus is dead." Acts 13:36, For David, after he had served his own generation by the will of God, fell asleep, was buried with his fathers. 1 Corinthians 15:51, Behold, I will tell you a Mystery: we shall not all sleep, and we shall be changed. 1 Thessalonians 4:13-14, Though I do not want you to be ignorant, brothers concerning those who have fallen asleep, lest you sorrow as others who have no hope. For when we believe that Jesus died and rose again, even so God will bring with Him those who sleep in Jesus. John 6:39-40, This is the will of the Father Who sent Me, that of all He has given Me I should lose nothing, and should raise it up the last day, and this is the will of Him Who sent Me, that everyone who sees the Son and believes in Him may have everlasting life; and I will raise **"him up"**, not (Her up) at the last day. Jesus, He is speaking to our spirit, not to our gender, and we shall all be changed. Let's say that a young married couple were born-again. She is 4'-8" tall, and her husband is 6'-2" tall, and they are coming from a family reunion. Grand-pa is driving and grand-ma is sitting next to him. (It must be an old automobile, I don't recall seeing a "bucket seat" for a very long time) The young couple are in the back seat, (The front seats are occupied) they are having a conversation, and in the blink of an eye, they were gone. (the rapture) Their spirits are going toward the Light, (Jesus) and their dead bodies is on the back seat with all their memories, dreams, hope, brain, etc. These two male spirits will not holdings hands, (This is not Hollywood) their focus as a spirit is to follow Christ, Who is that Light. They will not recognize each other either (They all will be changed). So, you see, it might be a fictional story, only it will happen exactly like that. When you die, your spirit is going to rest and go to sleep. John 5:25, Jesus is saying; "Most assuredly, I say to you, the hour is coming, and now is, when the dead will hear the voice of the Son of God; and those who hear will live." Verse 28-29, "Do not marvel at this; for the hour is coming in which all who are in the graves will hear His voice, and come forth, those who have done good to the Resurrection of Life, and those who have done evil, to the resurrection of condemnation."

Proverb 3:25-26, When you lie down (Most likely be dead), you will not be afraid; Yes, you will lie down, and your sleep will be sweet. (Because you are an "heir" with Jesus) Do not be afraid of sudden terror, nor of trouble from the wicked (Demon) when it comes; for the Lord will be your confidence, and will keep your foot from being caught. (Evil never gives up)

"Advertising is legalized lying"

(H. G. Wells) (1866-1946)

Many Evangelists and theologians do believe that Wisdom is actually Jesus. They believe that She didn't exist as a female Spirit, except that they always speak of Her as a female Spirit, only, they do not accept it as what She is—a female Spirit. The problem that I can see is that men have control on this world since the beginning. Women have no rights. When a woman husband died (Years ago) and had no offspring, she has (By the law of men) to marry her husband brother to give offspring to her dead husband; (What a crock) she has no saying in that matter. When a woman inherits from her father and was single, everything she have was transferred to the man she will marry, it was not her land or money no more it was her husband who becomes the owner of the land. Woman were in the "back seat" at all time ----since the beginning. Today, in a certain country, a woman living in a house and a man force himself into the home, and force himself into her, she is the guilty one because she brings shame in the family. (What a crock) She is the one who is guilty, and nothing happened to the man because he has needs. (What a crock) It is a men world, and we will tell you what to say and what to do. Men decided (Religious theologians and scholars) years ago that God, the Word, and the Holy Spirit were three, and they invented that word "Trinity" because they were three. What about Wisdom? She exists, they talk about Her in the Bible as a Female Spirit, and because of chauvinism from men, it is not acceptable that She will have a part of the "Trinity." There is just room for three, because of the word that they chose years ago. (Trinity) Today theologians and scholars do not want to find another word to replace "Trinity" for a fourth member in the family of God, so, She, cannot be a member of the family of God because She has no rights -- She is a female. Well, I personally say to all of you theologians and scholars; "Kiss my posterior" with your thinking. Jesus He is my Brother, my Shepherd, my Christ, my King, my Lord, and my Savior, and He is not my sister. As far as I am concerned, the family of God just became bigger. According to me the family of God is: **God the main Head, His Son the Word Who became flesh, the Holy Spirit, and Wisdom** Who is also Understanding. So, just to piss off the theologians today, I did find a new name **QUARTET.** I will say that the "Trinity has a fourth member now," and their new name is **QUARTET.** Put this in your pipe and smoke it. (Jesus, He is not my sister) Proverb 1:20, Wisdom call aloud outside; She raises Her Voice in the open squares. (She has a mouth) Proverb 3:16, Length of day are in Her right hand, in Her left-hand riches and honor. (She has hands) Proverb 4:9, She will place on your head an ornament of Grace; a crown of Glory She will deliver to you. (She has legs) Proverb 7:4, **Say to Wisdom," You are my sister".** How can Jesus be Her. Jesus, He is my Faith Brother, and He is not a "He/she", Jesus is not my sister. Jesus, He is my brother, and Wisdom, She is my sister. Wisdom is not a "fictional Spirit in our imagination. She is real, and She is the Wisdom of God. As Jesus, Who, is the Word of God, and the Holy Spirit is the Spirit of God. Also don't forget that Wisdom is the Understanding of God. Proverb 8:14, Counsel is Mine, and sound Wisdom; "I am Understanding" I have Strength (She has to be a real Spirit, She, got Strength). Proverb 8:22-31, "The Lord possessed Me at the beginning of His way, before His Work of old. I have been established from everlasting, from the beginning, before there was ever an earth. When they were no depths, I was brought forth, where they were no fountains abounding with water. Before the mountains were settled, before the hills, I was brought forth; while as yet He had not made the earth or the fields, or the primal dust (Human) of the world. When He prepared the Heavens, I was there, when He drew a circle on the face of the deep, when He established the clouds above, when He strengthened the fountains of the deep, when He assigned to the sea its limit, so that the waters would not transgress His command, when He marked the foundations of the earth, then I was beside Him as a One brought up, and I was daily His Delight, rejoicing always before Him, rejoicing in His inhabited world, and My delight was with the sons of men. These two words in your Bible master craftsman should be removed and replaced with as a "**One brought up**". It is impossible that God will use craft in His Works. Wisdom is a She, so, it is impossible that She is a "Master" and less a "Craftsman", She is a female Spirit, not a man, "per-say." Also, the **sons of men** it has to be put in there by theologians and scholars, and they knew that angels "nick-name" was sons of men. At that moment when Wisdom was speaking, the primal dust was not created yet, it doesn't make sense to me, that She will say "sons of men" because we (Primal dust) were not been created yet. She probably; said that My delight was with the angels of God. What a mess these theologians and scholars did over all these years, and it is there to stay. WHAT A MESS THEY DID, WHAT A MESS. Is it what I told you to be very careful at what you believe, and what you hear and read also. This is a good example for us to be aloof on everything we believe, especially in our reading. It's not because it is written that it is the Truth. (Check it out first). Proverb 3:24-25, When you lie down, you will not be afraid; yes, you will lie down and your sleep will be sweet. Do not be afraid of sudden terror, nor of trouble from the wicked when it comes. Because the wicked (Satan demons) will try to grab your spirit foot, and bring you in his "pit." Your guardian angel who will be watching over your spirit, and will tell the demon, do not touch **him**, **he** (Not her; sorry ladies) **is the Child of God**, and your sleep will be sweet. Proverb 19:23, The fear of the Lord leads to life, and **he** (Your spirit) who has it will abide in satisfaction; **he** (Not she) will not be visited with evil. Even in death, your spirit is protected from evil, and your sleep will be sweet. So, now you know that when you will be passing, that your spirit will not go to Heaven like your preacher preaches to you. Instead, it says he is going to sleep, until when **he** will hear the Voice of the Son of God, and wake up to go to the Light that is Christ. This is a powerful teaching for us who are still living and kicking in this world. After you did all your research you can go and show it to your preacher, and show him the real Truth about where we are going after we pass. All of you who like to argue because of your doctrine in your religion, do not come at me with your blah, blah, blah, I say to you, bring me the fact, and only the fact, and come back when you will have them, and good luck with that though. I will repeat some of the teaching. Wisdom is the only female Spirit to exist in the entire universe. I know that there is a lot of ladies who will be mad at me, and will have a hard time to believe that they are a **he** "spirit." It is God who is using the article **he, him**, it is not me, I am only the messenger. When you decided to not believe what I say, it means that you do not believe the Words of God; it was not my Words it was His. Go and complain to Him; He is the source, so, go to the source. It is impossible for God to lie or make mistakes also to have a doubt, and to sin. When God is using, he, him, my son, you will find out that He is speaking to our spirit, or to say it better, from Spirit to spirit.

"That which has always been accepted by

everyone, is almost certain to false"

Here is another "Nugget" for you to hear. When God is using the word "Possible" in His Word, it is impossible for Him to do that. I believe that it is these bad theologians and bad scholars who did it again. The word possible is a doubt word. Some of you might think that I am pushing the envelope, and I am going to far with this. The true meaning of that word, when you will go to a dictionary, and check it out, you will see that what the meaning of that word, the way they explain it, it is according to how the world speak. Open your mind when you will do your research and be careful, because it is a slippery slope. The word "possible is a "doubt" word when you are using it, and it is very hard to see for us, who speak it that word very often Ly. God willing, you will be able to see it more clearly, and you might think that I am not as stupid you thought I was in the first place. Think about the expression it's possible, it means that you do not know it yet, and you will find out later that it might happened, or might not might is a doubt. Its possible. The expression when possible is another one. You do not know when, only, you might know when, or you might not know when. The word possible is actually a question mark (??????), you don't know when, and do not know either is it possible. Or it means that "I am not sure". These expression words do not belong in the present and in the future tense; this is for sure. Change the way you speak, and instead of using these words, say it this way, "I don't know it yet". The way I see it, that it is not possible for God to use the word possible---period. How many times that we are using that doubt word in our conversation of every day? Do you know why that God it is impossible for Him to be using that word? It is because God knows everything in advance, so, it is impossible for God to say its possible. Here comes another "Fictional" story that you will like a lot. Let's say a preacher is reading and talking about what Luke 18:27, is saying. Luke 18:27, "The things which are impossible with men are possible with God". An older lady who is a new believer pay very much attention at what the preacher he is saying, because there is a part of her body that she didn't like very much. Her breasts are sagging, and she doesn't like that at all. So, she is paying very much attention about that, after all, is it possible that God can lift up these beautiful "puppy eyes" and make them look straight ahead again, that is what the Bible says, it must be true? (Will see) That night, going to bed, she started to talk to God about that. She heard that when you have a problem in your life that you can and should give it to God, He will take care of it. She praying about that and gave it to God, and started to believe with all her heart.

After that, she learned also that you have to say Thanksgiving prayers, and she continued to believe with all her heart that she already received what she is asking for. One month pass, and she continue to believe. Another month came to pass, and I started to wonder the famous question, "WHY" I did not receive it yet. She started to talk to some other ladies in her church, about her prayer that she asked God, and is surprise that she didn't receive it yet. One lady in the group said that she bought a book that explains clearly the "WHY" we do not receive sometimes. So, the lady takes the information about the book, and did go online, and she find the book and order it. Five days later, she received the book, and what a surprise she got when she is reading the "WHY" she didn't receive. The author was speaking about Luke 18:27, and explaining in the book that sometimes it is impossible for God to do it. The author was saying that God cannot break His Law, "**The Law of gravity**". Her breasts were getting heavier over the years, and it is normal that gravity was the problem. In a way, gravity was an enemy of her body. The Law of gravity of God our enemy, that a new one I've never heard that one before. You might think that this Normand he is a nut case, perhaps I am, only, I am a happy nut. So, now you know the name of that author, and that author he is very comfortable in his shoes. The Law of gravity is that, what's is up must go down, it is one of the Law of God and this Law is the Law of gravity. The author did tell the readers to go see a plastic surgeon, and he/she will do a very good job to make these beautiful "puppy eyes" to look straight ahead. He was explaining that to the readers that, the things that Luke 18:27 should be read this way:" The things that are impossible to men are a certainty to God". That lady did realize that the things that are impossible to God was a certainty to men. Personally, I believe that these bad theologians and bad scholars were involved in changing the Word of God for their own words. They really piss-me-off. They did it on purpose, to put doubts words coming from God's mouth. God's Words are Faith Words; there is no doubt in them, except when you are reading it, it looks like that He has doubts. (Did God change) These bad people are actually "WOLF" disguised as a sheep. They do not have God in their heart; they have "poison", and they are poisoning everyone when we are reading their words. Thank you to that plastic surgeon, you did a good job---they look great. Words that are a doubt: IF, MIGHT, BUT, PERHAPS, POSSIBLE.

"Truth never damages a

cause that is just"

When God did make a "Covenant" with Abram in Genesis 15:18, On the same day God made a Covenant with Abram….and up to the time when Jesus was living on this earth, it was known as the "Covenant," when they were speaking about the old time. When Jesus died and was Resurrected on the fourth day, He gave us His Will and Testament. Years later, these good theologians, as good as they try to be correct in their writing, because Jesus did give us a Testament when He died, they decided to call it the "New Testament". Not the New Covenant, and theologians and scholars they think that they are the cream of the crop. 500 years ago, or so, they decided to call the first Covenant, "Old Testament" even when blood was not shed to make it a testament. (What a mess they did) To call the (New) Covenant of God when Jesus died, the New Testament is wrong, it should be called the "New Covenant" because someone shed His blood to make it a Covenant. The first Covenant, nobody died, and no blood was shed, and no will was giving. When they call the second Covenant, the New Testament, they figure out that the first Covenant that is call Covenant, and the New Testament, it doesn't rime or it look funny in writing. So, the first Covenant was named "Covenant", and these religious peoples they didn't like that Covenant name, so, for certain, they will not call the new one "New Covenant". Because it will remind them too much of their fathers 4500 years earlier. So, they decided to call it the "New Testament" and we will call the first Covenant the "Old Testament" and at the same time, we do not need a reminder of what our fathers did, this probably, why they remove the word Covenant for Testament. Ease the pain. This is as hypocritical as it can be, only they didn't think that people will notice. Well, Normand did, and Normand said that they were wrong. Theologians and scholars, it is all about them, them, and them. They do not have in their hearts and minds, Christ, no, they don't, it is all about themselves. They do not give a "fart" about all the damage they did to us, and still continue doing so, and when they give a "fart" its "stinks" at what they did. Now we have that "Stench" for the last 600 years or more in our Bibles, and the worst thing is, the people believe everything what the Bible say. What a curse for us. You can see by now that I am not putting on some white gloves when I speak. Many people will not like the way I speak because I put them out of their "Comfort zone". It is not about me; it is all about you who want to grow, and I decided to give you the most precise teaching that I can give you. I want to wake up the one who is in a "Slump".

I will always speak the Words of God that He intended for us to hear, and speak it, and certainly not according to what the Bible is saying. God did tell us: "Be careful what's coming out of your mouth, and what's coming out of someone breath. Do not worry about what's coming out of my mouth, I will pay for what I say. God is fair, and the one who teaches the Word of God to be very aware that He is listening to your teachings, and He said that we will be more severely punished about what we are saying. I will pay like everyone else, maybe not as much though. It is about time that someone put his foot down. Doubts and unbelieve words, when you put them in your heart, you are putting yourself in jeopardy, outch. Mark 11:23, "For assuredly, I say to you, "Whoever says to this mountain, be removed and be cast into the sea, and does not doubt in his heart, and believes that those things **he** says will be done, **he** will have whatever he says. This is Jesus talking, and it is all about **he**. I am sure that Jesus knew that they will be millions of women born-again Christians. Do not worry about that, ladies God loves you too, and you will always be part of Him, when you will accept His Son as your "Personal Savior" in your heart, and God He is saying that you will be His Child. I will re-write for you Mark 11:23, according to Normand. "For assuredly, I say to you, whoever says to his/her mountain, be removed and be cast into the sea, and does not doubt in his/her heart, and believes that those things he/she says will be done, he/she will have whatever he/she says. Amen to that, sister. Verse: 24, Therefore I say to you, (Almost) whatever things you ask when you pray, believe that you receive them, and you will have them. It didn't work for the lady with the beautiful "puppy eyes", she was believing, except that her preacher did not have the same knowledge as other people have, so it is the people in the congregation who suffer. Hosea 4:6, My people are destroyed for lack of knowledge. It was not much of her fault; it was her preacher who had a lack of knowledge. You can remove the fault from the preacher's shoulder, and put them on the Denomination leaders. One way or another, everybody is losing. It will always be according to His Law for us to receive, and we cannot afford to having **a lack of knowledge.**

"Although you may tell lies, people will believe you, when only you speak with authority"

(Anton Chekhov) (1860-1904)

When you read the Apostles Gospels; you will find that they do not speak precisely like I do, it is because they do not have the same knowledge that I have about the Scripture, and they didn't have a condensed book like we have the Bible. So, I will let it slide, only, I understand why they wrote it like that, it is excusable. You cannot give the people information that you do not have in the first place; it is understandable. Mark 11:22, Jesus said; "Have the Faith **of** God." You will have to open your mouth to do this; you do not pray in your head, it doesn't work, you already know that because you didn't receive when you did pray in your head. God is saying; do it the same way I do, and you will be fine. When you have Faith in God, it is not the same. Even Satan and his demons believe that God exist, and they are shaking in their boots, that is when they have boots. Hebrew 10:23, Paul is saying; "Let us hold fast the confession of our hope (It should have said Faith, or believe, not hope) (Hope is for suckers) without wavering, for He Who promised is Faithful. You should replace the word "hope for believe". So, you should read it this way;" Let us hold fast the confession of our believe (Or Faith) without wavering, for He Who promised is Faithful" (That I like). Paul said; Let us hold fast the confession of our belief—and when you believe that you are healed, you are holding fast that belief. When you pray, the **problem** you will be holding fast your problem, and your problem will become bigger, and you will wonder **why that it looks like that my problem is becoming bigger.** The answer is; it is because you are still holding at your problem, that's why. This is why we have the expression: "Hell gets loose." Sometime we are our own enemy when we are using the word of our enemy. When we are holding fast to our prayer, and you did pray the problem, you are actually holding fast to your problem, because this is what you did pray for, and you don't even know it. Pray for the answer, and everything will be fine. So, what you should do now when you did learn your mistake, is to turn loose your problem prayer, and hold your confession when you will be praying the answer of your problem. Let's say that you name is Denise and you are reading in your "Personal Bible", that God wrote to you personally, and He is saying; "Whatever Denise say to her mountain (The problem) be thou removed, and you will have whatever you are asking Denise, as long that you believe with all your heart; and I am telling you My little one that you shall receive. You will have to use your mouth to do that; you cannot pray in your head, and expecting to receive; it is a no, no. Afterward, start to confess that you already received it, and give Me some of your most beautiful Thanksgiving prayers that I like, until you receive what you are asking Me---and I will do it for you, My little one.

Will it be nice to have a "Personal Bible" like that? What I am saying is that you can have it like that, you make it that way when you are reading His Words. Continue to believe with all your heart, and you will not miss on His promises that He has for you, and He is never wrong. Whatever your name is, make it personal to you, and you will come out a winner--- always. Words are the most powerful things in the universe; use it to your advantage. The devil knows it, and he wants you on his team. When I say to you about the unbelievers who do receive what they are saying with their mouth; (They do not pray God, they just don't believe in Him) and they believe with all their hearts, they receive what they are saying. Jesus said, **"You can have what you say." Many born-again do not know that, except Satan does, and he believes it.** Satan is limited about what he can do, so, he has to come on the scene, and distort our thoughts process, and when we agree with him, and believe his words---we are doomed. Satan cannot put words in your mouth, and in your heart, he has to find a way to do it. Satan already found a way to do that. Years ago, when he decided to start many religions and work with people who believed in that religion of his, and they became fanatics of that religion, it was easy after that for him to continue his dirty work. When, finally, the men of this world decided to make a Bible, guess who became involved in that project, you guessed it right, the theologians and scholars of many religions. This is one of his **many magical tricks** that he had, and people love magic tricks, except that magic is evil. When the devil did find his followers, he disguised them as sheep, and (Almost) everyone on this earth believes these religious fanatics as a good man of God. They are actually good man from this god, the god from this earth. Also, God himself cannot put His words in your mouth or in your heart, you will have to do it yourself. This is why He gives us choices; it is up to you to decide which words you want to put in it. He gave us the Prophets years ago; you are the one who has to **"Tattoo it"** in your heart -- His Word. When Jesus came and started Teaching "THE WAY" they didn't like it He was infringing on their believe, and on their religion, and they become scare to lose the power they had, so, they in Mark 15:11, Then the Chief Priests stirred up the crowd, and in Matthew 27:20, The Chief Priests and elders persuaded the multitudes, and they were screaming "That man is an impostor". That's what religion will do to you; it is to make you believe the wrong thing. God gives us the right to choose, so we choose Him or him, God's Word or men words.

> ## "An irreligious society cannot endure the truth
>
> ## of the human condition.
>
> ## It prefers a lie, no matter how idiotic it may be"
>
> ### (Nicholas Gomez) (1913-1994)

1 Peter 2:24, Who Himself bore our sins in His own body on the tree, (He didn't say on the cross, he said on the tree) that we, having died to sins, might live for Righteousness---by Whose stripe you were healed. Jesus did it 1992 years ago, and Peter said that you were healed, not that you will be healed, **that you are healed**. You just have to believe it with your Faith that you are already healed. When you leave your Faith in the "Drawer," (Your Faith may not be dusty, per-say; it is not strong though.) how can you expect to receive? **You have that Faith since you are born, so, use it, it will not bite you.** It is the same thing with a Bible when you stash it away, you make yourself prisoner of yourself. Use it, it is for your own good, do not "Handcuff" yourself, free yourself for the best to come. When you pray, ask God, **not Jesus.** Jesus said in John 16:23, and in that day (After the Resurrection) you will ask Me nothing. Most assuredly, I say to you, whatever you ask My Father in My Name, He will give you what you are asking. We have to pray to the Father, and Jesus said; I will do it. Also, I am going to the Father, do not ask Me nothing. Well, a lot of people are asking Jesus to heal them, I am wondering what kind of preachers they have in these churches (Not a good one, I guess). Let's say that one person will have a sickness in his/her body, in 8 months from now, it is a serious disease. Well, Jesus already healed that person, even when that person will receive that sickness in his/her body in 8 months from now, that person is already healed. Jesus said it by His stripes that we're healed, not that we will be healed. 1992 years ago, you were healed, and 8 months later, sickness appeared in your body, and with all the information that you have now, you know now, since the Resurrection that was 1992 years ago + 8 months later, you know that you are healed already, when it will happen. This is what the devil does to test our Faith. He will put disease in your body, and step aside and watch what you will do with that situation. You have to use your faith, that same Faith when you were a little child. Did your preacher told you exactly the same way I am teaching you, to

"How to go" and get that blessing of yours that it is already yours. Did he remind you to ask the Father and not Jesus? What about the Thanksgiving prayers? Did he talk about that to his congregation? Did he know that you are already healed, or he said Let's pray Jesus. You do not need to stay in that kind of church when the preacher does not do what he is supposed to do. You are the one who pays for **his lack of knowledge.** This is why Jesus said to us, **"Do not ask Me anything", I already said it on the tree, "It is finished." So, I am not going back on that tree again, you understand, "It is finished", ask My Father, and in My Name; I will do it.** Lot of born-again speak the words of the enemy, they are speaking the same way as the world speaks. They do not pay attention at what's coming out of their mouth. They just don't. Ex: I am sick, I'm broke, I think I'm getting the cold. It might be all true**, just don't say it.** When you speak the problem, you are not speaking the answer, you are talking about the problem. Philippians 4:19, My God shall supply all my need according to His riches in Glory by Christ Jesus. People will sometimes, after being asked, do you believe that you are heal, and that person will answer," I hope so". Hope has no substance, so don't waste your time with it—it is for suckers. We have to be careful (Personally, I am careful with my words, except I am using some harsh words sometimes, just to shake you up) with our tongue; it can Bless you or destroy you. When you can control that tongue of yours, you will be controlling your whole body also. The devil cannot do anything on you without your authorization or your consent. Yes, he did put it there (In your body) only, you are the one who decided to keep it as "yours now". The devil will try to make something stick in you, and to make you believe that actually you are getting the cold. So, be aware of how you feel, see, touch, taste, hear, and beware of his make-believe tricks. Words are the most powerful things on this earth for us, and with no-action of your part = nothing. **Faith with work on your part = success in your life.** As powerful as those words are coming out of our mouth, action will speak the loudest.

Do your words are important.

(In the affirmative, God will say; let them flow, in the negative the devil will say; let them flow.)

Matthew 12:34-37, Broods of vipers! How can you, being evil, bring forth good things; for out of the abundance of the earth the mouth speaks? A good man/woman out of the good treasure of his/her heart brings forth good things, and an evil man/woman out of the evil treasure brings forth evil things. I say to you that every idle word man/woman may speak, they will give account of it in the day of judgment. For by your words, you will be justified, and by your words you will be condemned. There is "Power" in the Words of God, also, there is power in the words of the devil, and there is power in your own words, when you decide which words you want to believe. The Words that are coming from the Kingdom of God, or the words coming from the "pit" where evil resides—you chose. This is why that God said that words are very powerful in both worlds, His world or our world. This is why that God wants us to engrafted His Word in our heart, only, lot of people decided to tattoo the words of fears and doubt in their hearts. I will never repeat it enough, that words are the most powerful things in both universes. The words of the law in your country are very powerful. The words of your boss are very powerful, you better to listen to them or he/she will remind you who is the boss. There is "Power" in words, and it is a "Force", so they can be "Powerful" in your life. That force can bring you up, or bring you down--- you are the one who really decides which power you want in your life, his words or His Words (Words are invisible, and are a force). When you hear someone speak, it comes from his/her heart, that person did put it in his/her heart on their own accord. No other one's put these words there except yourself. When your heart overflows it, it is what will come out of your mouth. You are the only one who put it there. You cannot blame your parents, teacher, preacher, neighbor, spouse, etc., you are the one who is responsible of what's in your heart, and you are responsible for your words you speak. It is all about the "Thinking". When you think something and believe in your heart, this is where it goes. Same thing with the mind also, (It just like a fart, you heard it, and now it's gone.). So, when you are thinking right or wrong, and you will believe it, it is what you will speak, you will be right or wrong. You cannot have any doubt(s) you have to believe it at 100%. When you have only one doubt, you are believing 99%. You may think; that's close enough, except no, not to God. He said to believe with all your heart, all means 100%. It is up to you to decide how to live your life, and when you choose "Fear words" instead of Faith words, unbelief words instead of belief words. When you will see that your life is in shambles, there is a good chance that you will rethink the thinking of yours and change the way you speak. God **creative Power** comes from His mouth, and He said to us," Be like Me". You want to be a powerful born-again Christian, do like Him then. When you speak fear words that came from your mouth that come from your heart, will you say that this mistake will be compounded? When you speak blessed words (Righteousness) that come from your mouth that came from your heart, will you say that this Blessing will be compounded? Fear words create fear situations. Can you see it now that you are a creator with your own words, and can also destroy your own life with your words? Jesus told us 1992 years ago that we are healed, and people do not believe it. (Sad and true) You can be by yourself, and pray to God when sickness appear in your body (Myself **I do not allow it to come**), and that beautiful machine of ours can heal itself, when you believe that you are already healed, and go get that healing of yours by Faith, from the fourth dimension where God's Spirit is, and bring it in the third dimension where you live. That you have a minor or major problem, you can handle it on your own, (I did it many years ago, and still doing it) and you can ask someone to pray with you, it's double the Faith, double who will say Thanksgiving prayers, **it's double The Power.** Everything produces after its kind. An oak tree will have an oak tree, a pine tree will have a pine tree, a rabbit will produce another rabbit, a human will produce another human, a monkey will produce another monkey, and not a human, as Darwin is saying. Faith will produce Faith answer, and fear will produce after its own kind, fear itself.

"Sin has many tools, and a lie is the handle which fits them all"

(Oliver W. Holmes) (1809-1894)

When the Word of God is absent, Faith is absent; when your own words are absent, Faith is absent. When you are praying in your head, you will never receive what you are saying in your head, because your inside ears, doesn't count. You have to use your own mouth, and hear your own words with your outside ears, and when you will believe what you are hearing, and believe it with all your heart, God said; "Thou shalt receive according to your heart." You will not receive it yet, you will have to go get it with your Faith, and Thanksgiving prayers, and bring it (That Blessing) to you in the third dimension, where you live. These prayers are not something you say and receive right away; no, no, you have to work at it, with all your heart, you cannot wait for God for you to receive. Faith demands actions also, for us to receive, and laziness will get you nowhere with that. James 3:10, Out of the same mouth proceed Blessing and cursing. We have to establish God's Word here on earth, and one of the biggest problems for God and for us also is that we have been establishing the words of the enemy, the devil. When we bound (Put some restrain) God, because we are speaking the words of the enemy, God cannot help you when you are asking Him to help you, because He cannot break His own Law, when He said: "Anything you ask, believe that you already received, and thou shalt receive. So, when you speak the wrong words, God already said it, that you will also receive. Pay attention when you speak; your words are the most powerful things in the universe. When you speak the word of the enemy, God has no choice, only to stand aside, and let you receive when you will say for Ex: It doesn't work, I'm sick, I think I am getting the cold, having doubts when you pray, I'm broke, I'm afraid of, that diet of mine is no good, I'm dying to see that new movie, I'll fear that, I'm afraid my health is declining, etc. etc. **Pride is something that God despised the most**; it is the most hidden sin of all. **Pride is the patriarch of all sins,** the oldest. Do you know about the Power of binding and loosing? Matthew 18:18, Jesus is saying, "Assuredly, I say to you, whatever you bind on earth will be bound in Heaven, and whatever you loose; on earth will be loosed in Heaven. Matthew 16:29, I will give you the Keys of the Kingdom of Heaven, and whatever you bind---that is, declare to be improper and unlawful---on earth must be bound in Heaven; and whatever you loose, on earth---declare lawful---must be what is already loosed in Heaven. I will paraphrase some Words of Jesus. I will give you believers Authority and Power to loosen things on this earth that are allowed in Heaven, and that you can bind things on this earth that are not allowed in Heaven. We need to find out what things are not allowed in Heaven? Evil thoughts, disease, no lack of any kind, poverty, sickness, etc. What are the things that can be loosed in Heaven? Happiness, peace, a healthy body, and Eternal Life. So, what Jesus is saying is: That we have authority to bind evil forces on the earth, bind also poverty, sickness, and even sin that comes from the evil forces. We can, and we should loosen in Heaven all that is also very important in our born-again Christian Life. The word of the devil can release "Death" into you. The Word of God can release LIFE into you. Deuteronomy 30:12-14, It is not in Heaven, that you should say, who will ascend into Heaven for us and bring it to us, that we may hear it and do it? Nor is it beyond the sea, that you should say, who will go over the sea for us and bring it to us, that we may hear it and do it? Although the Word is very near you, in your mouth and in your heart, that you may do it. One way to learn is for you to research the promises of God in the Bible that are for us believers. Say them to yourself and believe them; and what will happen is that you will build them into your spirit, and continue to declare them these

Promises of yours, and you will see it after a period of time that these Promises who are the Truth from God, will become build into your spirit and they will become true for you, and in you. It will not come overnight, these Blessings Promises, you really have to work at it to put them in your heart. When life will trough you a "Curve ball" and you will swing at it, and you will not miss because you already know the answer, and know what to say to that "Curve ball." (Bad situation) Because you already did teach your spirit with the Word of God, and God did say; "Thou shalt receive." You might need money for a car, clothes, groceries, mortgage, and when it will happen, you already know that the Bible says that; Philippians 4:19, "My God has supplied all my need according to His riches by Christ Jesus." You just have to believe it, that those Words are for you to receive, and you will receive according to your heart, not according because of your feelings, when you will be in a bad situation, and you're thinking that God will give it to you, because you are His Child. God He is not moved by our emotions; **He will do it only according to your heart, and not according to your tears.** You really have to teach your spirit, do not listen to what your body wants, your spirit should be in charge of your body, and not your body in charge of your spirit. Continue to watch your sports, or your movies every night, and when that "Curve ball" will come (Evil are **always** watching), and when you will try to handle it, your body who is in charge will not be able to help you, because the one who can help you, (Your spirit) he is in a slump somewhere in your body, because you didn't teach yourself the Promises of God, for yourself in a moment of needs. Keep saying to your mouth these Promises up to the times that they become a part of you, and you'll see that they will become a Truth in you. John 15:7, "When you abide in Me, and My Words abide in you, you will ask what you desire, and it shall be done for you." In verse 8, "By this My Father is Glorified, that you bear much fruit; so, you will be My Disciples." All this is for you to receive according to your heart. When you will have a problem and didn't teach your spirit, well, just go and ask that famous team of yours or the famous player to help you in your moment of need. Or ask that famous movie star that you like a lot for help, and you will find no answers coming from them.

"Coming out of some mouths, the truth itself smells bad"

These are some of His Promises that come from the mouth of Prophets, Apostles, Wisdom, Jesus, and they are all His Words, it is up to you to believe them, and teach them to the real you---that is your spirit. Deuteronomy 28:1-14, I will let you read it for yourself, as God will be speaking to us today. When God says to Israel; "The increase of your herds, the increase of your cattle." Personally, you can think about your "Business" that you have. It could be more employees, and a much more production for your business to be successful. Also, "The offspring of your flocks." You will see it as your children's -- children's; or more people working for you. Also, "In your storehouses." Could be your bank account, the bigger the better---right? So, you can read it with your eye's glasses of today, not with the eye's glasses of 5000 years ago. Open your mind, and see all that Blessing is in there for you ---today. Psalm 37:4, Delight yourself also in the Lord, and He shall give you the desires of your heart. 1 John 4:4, You are of God, little children, and have overcome them, because He Who is in you is Greater than he who is in the world. James 4:7, Therefore submit yourself to God. Resist the devil, and he will flee from you. Psalm 119:89, Forever O Lord Your Word is settled in Heaven, and I will be established on earth when you speak His Words. Galatians 3:13-14, Christ has redeemed us from the curse of the Law, having become a curse, for us, that the Blessing of Abraham will come upon the Gentiles in Christ Jesus, that we will receive the Promise of the Spirit through Faith. Romans 8:11, When the Spirit of Him Who raised Jesus from the dead dwells in you, He Who raised Christ from the dead will also give Life to your mortal bodies through His Spirit Who dwells in you. Matthew 16:19, I will give you the Keys of the Kingdom of Heaven, and whatever you bind on earth will be bound in Heaven, and whatever you loose; on earth will be loosed in Heaven. 1 Corinthians 12:27, Now you are the body of Christ, and members individually. (We are a member of many members of the Body of Christ). Isaiah 54:17, No weapon formed against you shall prosper. Psalm 1:1-3, Blessed is the man/woman who walks not in the counsel of the ungodly, nor stands in the path of sinners, nor sits in the seat of scornful; and his/her delight is in the Law of the Lord, and in His Law he/she meditates day and night. He/she shall be like a tree planted by the rivers of water, that brings forth its fruit in its season, whose leaf also shall not wither; and whatever he/she does shall prosper. Psalm 54:13, All your children shall be taught by the Lord, and great shall be the peace of your children. 2 Corinthians 8:9, For you know the Grace of our Lord Jesus Christ, that though He was rich, yet for your sakes He became poor, that you through His poverty will become rich. John 10:10, The thief the devil does not come except to steal, and to kill, and destroy. I have come so they may have Life, and that they may have it abundantly. Philippians 4:13, I can do all things through Christ Who strengthens me. Ephesians 6:16, Above all, taking the shield of Faith with which you will be able to quench; all the fiery darts of the wicked one. James 1:22, Be a doer of the Word, and not hearers only, deceiving yourselves. Luke 6:38, Give, and it will be given to you; good measure, pressed down, shaken together, and running over will be put in your bosom. For with the same measure that you use, it will be measured back to you. (You are the one who has to give first, and it will be given to you) James 1:5, When any of you lack Wisdom, let him/her ask of God, Who, gives to all liberally and with reproach, and it will be given to him/her. 2 Corinthians 9:6-8, This I say: He/she who sows sparingly will also reap sparingly, and he/she who sows bountifully will also reap bountifully. Philippians 4:19, My God shall supply all your need according to His riches in Glory by Christ Jesus. Ephesians 4:29-30, Let no corrupt word proceed out of your mouth, except what is good for necessary edification, that it may impart Grace to the hearers. Do not grieve the Holy Spirit of God, by Whom you were sealed for the Day of Redemption. 1 John 5:4-5, For whatever is born of God overcomes the world. This is the Victory that has overcome the world---your Faith. Who is he/she who overcomes the world, only he/she who believes that Jesus is the Son of God. Romans 5:17, For when by one man's offense (Adam) death reigned through the one, much more those who receive abundance of Grace, and of the Gift of Righteousness will reign in Life through the One, Jesus-Christ. Proverb 3:5-6, Trust in the Lord with all your heart, and lean not on your own understanding; in all your ways acknowledge Him, and He shall direct your path. Psalm 119:105, Your Word is a lamp to my feet, and a Light to my path.

"It takes a minute to tell a lie,

and an hour to refute it"

(Noam Chomsky) (1928 --------)

Some people sometimes will tell you; the devil just won't let me do what I want to do today, he's only on my back. Who said that the devil is on your back? ----Oh, It was-myself. You receive what you say, and give power to the devil to using your mouth. You cannot have a conversation with the voice in your head. When you did pray for something and 6 weeks later you did not receive yet, the voice in your head will tell you; it doesn't work, yeah, you're right, it doesn't work. You even say that the devil is so smart, he doesn't give me a break, and he is always a step ahead of me, and he is putting a stick in my wheel that I try to build for my family. Who says that to you? (The devil) Thinking it over, you probably will say; It was me; I say that to myself. You will find out that your biggest enemy was your own mouth. Are you saying that the devil is smarter than the God in you? The thing is that Satan cannot be everywhere; he needs to have someone to help him. Evil is always watching; they know you; better than yourself. They heard when you speak when you are impatient, the voice in your head is a demon, he is the one doing havoc in you. Matthew 12:37, Jesus said; "For by your words you will be justified, and by your words you will be condemned."(Be careful about that statement, do not take it literally) It doesn't mean that you cannot be in Heaven, it just that a certain reward that was supposed to go to you will go to somebody else, and you will still be saved. Romans 3:3-4, For what when some do not believe? Will their unbelief make the Faithfulness of God without effect? Certainly not! Indeed, let God be True and every man/woman a liar. As it is written in Psalm 51:4, "That you may be justified in your words, and blameless when you are judged." When you will get in front of Him, and the books will be open, you will find and fast enough, when your own words did say, because everything is recorded, and your words will be judging you, because of who you believe- - -the Words of God or the words of a man. (Religion) Lot of people swallow everything they hear, especially when they see that so many people believe everything, it has to be true. It is almost impossible that so many can be wrong. So, it has to be true. (And they are wrong) Also, laziness this is one of the biggest enemies of our body. Some will believe the biggest lie from the mouth of the enemy, and will not consider giving a chance to God to show them the real Truth. Even some members of my own family who are born-again for at least 40 years believe that the Bible is accurate 100% or almost. When they will be able to read this book, will I lose them? The bad theologians and bad scholars they put so much garbage in every book in the New Covenant. I told you before, these yack-ass they really piss me off. Our body it so well done, it is a beautiful machine that can heal itself. That you believe in God or do not know Him, start to believe by Faith with all your heart, and they can receive the Blessing that God has for everyone.

(You will never here this in any churches in this world. You will receive according to your heart, and God cannot stop you from receiving when you are doing everything by the book. (When you are His Child, or not) Here is another beautiful "Fictional" story for you. A man said to his wife that he had a pain in his left side of his body. When he touched it, it hurt, and she said; let's make an appointment to see the doctor. They are both born-again Christians, except that they never did use their Faith. Doctor takes an X-ray, and he tells them to come back in two weeks. When they enter the office again, they sit down with the doctor. Putting the X-ray on the wall, he said; do you see that mass in here, they said yes, well, he said it is cancer. The man said; "I can't believe I got cancer," and looking at his wife, he said; "I got cancer." What can I do, doctor? The doctor said you will have to do something about that, etc. (End of the story) I will tell the same story with a few changes in it. A man who is married and they are both born-again Christians, except that his wife never uses her Faith, but her husband he is always using his Faith. He has the same pain, made two appointments, and finally, they are in the doctor office. So, the doctor said; do you see that mass in here, they both said yes, and the doctor said; well, Sir, you have cancer. The man says--no I don't, the doctor looks in the direction of the lady and wonders. So, he said to the man Is this your name on the right corner of the X-ray? The man says, yes, it is. The doctor said Is this your SSN#, yes, it is. The doctor said; Sir, you have cancer, and the man replied No, I don't. The doctor said; You better to do something about that, and the man said, I already did something about that. I refuse to admit that it is mine. Walking in the parking lot, he started to speak to God and start believing that he was already healed.(End of the story)

"There are 2 ways to be fooled. One is

to believe what isn't true; the other

is to refuse to believe what is true"

(Soren Kierkegaard) (1813-1855)

Let me explain something. When someone rings the bell, and a man is outside with a package, and you answer the door, he says; is this your name on that

that package, you say yes. I need your signature, and you sign it, and he gives the package; and said; its all yours. Think about the first man in the story who has that "Package;" in his body. He said 2 times, I got cancer, with his mouth, and he just signed that "Package", (With his mouth) it's all yours now, you can keep it. It is the devil who put it there, and because you didn't know how it works with God Faith, you can keep that package; it's all yours. (It's sad) The second story that man has that "Package" only, he refused to admit that it is "His package" and never signed that package with his mouth. Same story with two different endings. It doesn't mean that because you have that package in your body that it is yours, and you have to keep it. No, no, no, no, no. This is sad to say, only when you will go to these born-again churches, there are a lot of sick parishioners. This is all around the world in all Denominational churches. **My people are dying for lack of knowledge.** There should be more and more teaching in these churches. When God does a "Miracle" that person receives right away, it is a Faith Miracle. Miracles do not happen too often, so we have to go with our Faith and Thanksgiving prayers, normally. It is what it is. God He is hearing your request, and at the same time He is looking in your thoughts, and looking in your heart. This is one of the most important teachings; that you should pay attention to it, your mouth, your thoughts, and your heart have to go together in unison. Faith is something that you are born with; your Faith that you will use it or not, will always be the same size. In many churches, the preacher said that the more you are using your Faith, the bigger it becomes. This is a lie. God did say: that your Faith is becoming **stronger**, not bigger. This is what religious people say, and these born-again preachers they just speaking the same way as the world speaks. **Be careful what's coming out of your mouth- --period.** You are the one who has to change, when everything is not going the way; it should be. Some people will not like it to hear the way I speak, and when I say so many things the way I say it, and they will have a hard time believing all that. (Go to the source, God. Some of you do not go and ask your preacher, he most likely never heard this before, so, he cannot tell you what he doesn't know) They probably even say that it is understandable to say; I got cancer when the package is in my body. I will say to them; you are mistaken, Sir, ma'am. They probably will say that I am stupid, I will say to you who believe like that, I like better to be stupid with a healthy body, than to be sick, and listen to these flapper mouths who think that they are right. Remember what I said earlier. When you are right and act on your thinking, you will be right. When you are wrong and act on your thinking, you will be wrong. When you think stupidly and you act on your stupidity, you will be stupid. So, do some drastic changes the way you speak.

Proverb 4:20-22, Wisdom is saying; My child, pay attention to My Words; incline your ears to My saying: Do not let them depart from your eyes; keep them in the midst of your heart; (Tattoo) for they are life to those who find them, and health to all their flesh. Proverb 3:8, Do not be wise in your own eyes; fear the Lord and depart from evil. It will be Health to your flesh, and Strength to your bones. These proverbs were written 4000 years ago, and these words are still keeping the same Power today. Matthew 10:32-33, Therefore, confess Me before men, him/her I will also confess you before My Father Who is in Heaven. Whoever denies Me before men, him/her I will also deny before My Father Who is in Heaven. Many, I will say: "Fake: born-again do not want people to know that they are not a born-again. (They are spy) So, you see, you can deny Jesus; only by your non-action on your part, and Jesus said, I will deny you too, to My Father.

"Truth is what's left when

You run out of excuses"

(Marty Rubin) (1930—1994)

The most significant problem I see for a born-again person is to believe the unbelieved words and how the world speaks it. Ex." It doesn't work" are his favorite words for us to hear. The voice in your head, like I say, he is an idiot, we all know that by now. When you did say a prayer to God for you to receive, evil is there to watch us, and he wants you to fail. Demons working for Satan, they know that it will take time to receive, because we have to go with our Faith, and it will take time for us to receive, and these demons they know all of that. They are watching us like a hawk, and we are their prey. They can see that we become impatient also, so the voice in your head will say to your spirit, time and time again, "It doesn't work, it doesn't work". After hearing it so many times, it is just a matter of time before we start to say it yourself," it doesn't work", and we are doomed. You might even say," I do not know why God do not want to give me my request. How can you receive now, when God He is reading your heart, and heard what you just said. Most likely we don't even know it **why**, the answer is lack of knowledge it is as simple as that, we are speaking the words of the enemy. The unbelief people they never thought to ask God, because He doesn't exist to them.

They believe with all their heart, also they will never hear that voice in their head, saying," it doesn't work, because they are already in the "Hell wagon," this is why they receive faster than us born-again Christians. All these bad expressions coming from the devil that we are hearing in our head, well, them, they don't. They are the lucky one---are they really lucky? It is not easy to be a born-again and walk with God, and not have all these challenges coming to us. Proverb 6:2, You are snared by the words of your mouth; you are taken by the words of your mouth. Written 4000 years ago, and so much is true. These Words from the Wisdom of God are working for you or against you. We have to be careful what we are saying, and really pay attention at what is coming out of our mouth, it is not easy in a way, only, we have to fight the good fight of Faith. (1 Timothy 6:12) When we don't like the way people act sometimes, we say: "These people make me sick." Did you hear that? WOW. It is contrary to God's Word, or am I mistaken? Not too long after that, when we are repeating the same expression again and again, and we find ourselves sick, and we don't even know "why." We are not paying attention at what's coming out of our mouth, and we thought that we we're not speaking as the world speaks. Change the way you speak, and you will have a healthy body also. That you realize it or not, these words will do their job. You are saying that you are "sick," and God said; Thou shalt receive according to your heart, outch. Or you might say, I'm just "dying" to go see that new movie. This thing is just tickling me "to death." The devil did programme our language of everyday for the last 6000 years and counting. He wants us to speak his words, and not the Words of God. In a way, we are our own enemy, our own mouth is working against us---WOW I did not know that how severe it is--- now you know, what will you do with all this information? (It's not time to be lazy) Will see. Job 3:25, Job said; "**For the things I greatly feared** came upon me." What happened to Job came all at once from the devil's work. We can see that it was in his mind, (Job) that it will happen to him, and he probably believed it with all his heart that one day something will happen to him. Well, he received according to his heart --- all the thing I greatly feared. He never did give up; he did continue to fight, the good fight -- and Victory came. When you put Faith in action, doing the talk and the walk, you will bring God on the scene. When you have "Fear" in action, you will bring the devil on the scene, doing a lot of talk, and no walk. Fear will always bring more fear into your life. Talk Blessing, and you will bring more Blessings to yourself, to your body, to your business, and to your immediate family also. Proverb 10:31-32, "The lips of the Righteous know what is acceptable, and the mouth of the wicked what is perverse," and what is perverse? When speaking the words of Satan, it is perverse to God, and should be perverse to us also; wrong is wrong. It is not acceptable to God. What it means is when you are Righteous, it is because you are doing the right thing, that is speaking the Words of God, and it is "acceptable." When we don't like the way our city government runs the city, sometimes we will say; that they are a "Bunch of idiots. When the city is going in shambles, (We did prophesize on this) and more in shambles, no wonder why everything is the way it is, we are saying it, and believe it, and God said thou shalt receive. I speak like that myself, and many times, so you are not the only one---oops. What we should do is to go to Joshua, he was the one who replaced Moses after he passed. It was a long time ago, and God's Words are as much Powerful today as they were yesterday. Joshua 1:8-9, **This Book of the Law shall not depart from your mouth (Our mouth too), and you shall meditate in it day and night, that you may observe to** do according to all that is written in it. For then you will make yourself prosperous, and then you will have good success. Have I not commanded you; be strong and of good courage; do not be afraid, nor be dismayed, for the Lord your God is with you wherever you go.

"Night is for the thieves,

Light is for the truth"

(Euripides) (496-406 BC)

That you speak God's Words or the words of the devil's you did succeed in bringing one or the other into your life because your words are the most powerful things in the universe. Sometimes, as a born-again Christian, when we speak God's Words and also the words of His enemy; we are wondering, why is it that God seems like He doesn't hold my hand right now? God is a jealous God; He will not hold our hand when we are speaking perverse things. (Devil words) Word produces after its own kind. **You speak success words, success you will receive. You speak fear and doubt words; it is what you will receive, fear and doubts.** Proverb 12:17-19, "He who speaks truth declares Righteousness, and the false witness (Antichrist) deceit. The Words of God are True Words, and the devil's words have no truth in it. There is One Who speaks like a piercing of a sword, and the tongue of the wise promotes health. The Truthful lip shall be established forever, and a lying tongue is only for a moment."

This is not as easy-peasy as we will think for us to start to change the way we speak. It demands a lot of effort, and most likely, people will do nothing, because when laziness is comfortable in your body, it is hard to do things. You really have to do some effort because you are going to be sleeping for good one day, and we cannot assume that we will live a very old life, we have to prepare ourselves, we have to think about the future, we know that the future sometimes it is uncertain. Be aware of all that. I say to you, **you want to do nothing, so be it then. You want to be sick, so be it then. You want to be in want, so be it then.** You do not want to change, because of all that work that you will have to do---don't then. Do not come and complain that your life is in shambles, or it's going in the drain. God give us the right to choose—choose wisely then. You chose a certain way to live your life the way you see fit, so be it, you got what you want---nothing. The devil will come after your finances, touch your healthy body, and steal so many years of your life. (Not because he hate's you; he hate's everyone—live with it, or fight the good fight) When a person dies at 82 years of age, the devil steals 38 years from that person life, because we should be able to live up to 120 years in here. When the devil attacks our Faith, and we let him do it, and when you speak his words at all time (That you know it or not) you might live on Eternity on Eternity with him, even when you did accept Jesus as your personal Savior, when Jesus will read your heart when you show up at the gate, Jesus will say; I do not know you depart from Me, outch. You decide. God is "**THE**" Provider, and when we are in want, and using His Word with our mouth, and plant a seed, you will have a "harvest". When you do not plant no seeds, how can you expect to receive a harvest? So, what God is saying is; when you will speak My Words, and I can see that you really want it (He is reading our heart), I will make sure that it is performed, according to your heart---off course. Proverb 13:2, "A man/woman should eat good by the fruits of his/her mouth; and the soul of the transgressor shall eat violence." The transgressors are the one who speak like the devil speaks, and these people cannot, and do not have the Words of God in them. I will repeat myself in here, because it has to be heard again, and again. James 1:26-27, "When anyone among you, who thinks he/she is religious, and does not bridle his/her tongue, and deceives his/her own heart, this one's religion is useless. Pure and undefiled religion before God and the Father is this: To visit orphans and widows in their trouble, and to keep oneself unspotted from the world." Like I said, and I will repeat it, I do not believe that James said that. It smells too much like religion to me. Theologians and scholars are not to be trusted whatsoever. It said that religion is useless; to God, any religion is useless.

That religious comment that they made years later, these religious persons are actually hitting on their own religion, they are digging themselves a hole --- what a loser. Pure and defiled religion, that is no good for them either, according to God, religions are not pure, and are defiled, it doesn't make sense, why someone will write like that? I know, it wasn't James; he was not a religious man. It will not surprise me that it was written in the year 1465, around that period. It did not come from the Holy Spirit; that statement, and God never actually wrote a book. The two things that I recall are that He wrote the Ten Commandments, and Moses did break's the tablets in pieces. The second time is when the finger of God was written on the wall of a palace. The Holy Spirit gave an account of what happened in the beginning, and gave it to Moses, and he wrote the first 5 books from our Bible, they are called. (The Pentateuque) Since his writing has been diluted, every time they have decided to rewrite the New Bible every 150 years or so. How many times that the Word of God been diluted, you think, 10 times? I don't know. In 150 years from now, they will change it again, because they will say; we do not speak like that no more.

"Truth gives a short answer,

while the lie usually babbles"

(German proverb)

In 1465, a Bible showed up out of the press, and in 1604, King James decided to rewrite it because the Bible they were using was so corrupt, these religious people asked King James to do something about that. That Bible, which was so corrupt, was not written by a plumber or a tile worker; it was written by theologians and scholars, and it was corrupt. Tell me something I don't know. In 1611, the Authorized King James Bible was out of the press. All these 50 theologians and scholars decided to change also the Word that God had already spoken years earlier. They decided to make God to start to talk like us. So, they put doubts word in the mouth of God; they added the word IF, MIGHT, POSSIBLE, PERHAPS, BUT, in His mouth. What they were saying without saying it; We (Theologians) do not want to speak His Word, so, will make Him speak our words, and God speak just like us now. **They really piss-me-off.** I know for a fact that every Word of God are Faith Words, and that there are no doubts in it, except that when I am reading His Word today, well, **I'm not so sure now? Is He the same as yesterday? I'm not sure, it seems that He has doubts when He speaks to me in the Bible. Did He change and did not tell us? I am confused! When you speak to God, you cannot have any doubts in your request; only when He speaks to us in our Bibles, He has doubts coming from His mouth.** When you are reading the Bible today, you are reading the words of men. Not the Word of God as He intended for us to hear. God will never use an "IF" when He speaks ---never. When you will be in the front of God, and He asks you that question; "Did you believe My Words, or you believe what men wrote in the Bible as My Words. You probably will wonder, is my name in that Big Book over there, is my name is in the "Book of Life"? You might say to God; "It was stupid of my part, I didn't know". God will say to you: "**Stupidity is not an excuse**" I saw you putting your Bible those men wrote, and put it on your chest, and crossing your both arms and said; I believe every thing that is in this Bible." God will continue and say: "You made your choice to follow what the words of men say, instead of Mine." OK, it was only a fictional story, and that story will make you think a little bit down the road, and scare you. Indeed, let God be True and every man/woman a liar. Psalm 51:4, This is what David was saying to God: "Against You; You only, have I sinned, and done this evil in Your sight." That You may be Justified when You speak, and be clear when You judge." All these bad theologians and bad scholars, and bad teachers of the Word of God will say; "Against You; You only, when we decided to believe men's words, and do this evil in Your sight. The way of a "fool" is right is his/her own eyes. Are you that "Fool" that Wisdom is talking about? When you decided to believe everything what men put in the Bible, that they are the true words. Be careful to believe the words of men as an actual truth. (God did say that every, men are liars)

"Have courage when you tell the

truth, you will never go wrong"

(Sophocles)

Luke 6:46, "Why do you call Me Lord, Lord, and not do the thing that I say"? Jesus wants us to be like His Father. To talk like Him, to act like Him, to think like Him, to pray like Him, to walk like Him, to believe like Him, to be Perfect like He is Perfect. This is why Jesus said: Why are you calling Me Lord, Lord, and not do what I say? Jesus when He was tempted by the devil, always responded with: "It is written," and it was the Word of God that Jesus was quoting to the devil. They were not too much words of the devil in the "old manuscript." The devil is the god on this earth, and everyone who came on this earth, and has the blood of Adam in them; God says that all men/women are liars. Satan did find a way to put his words in the Bible, and make people to believe that it is the words of God, outch. Today, when we say: "It is written" when reading the Bible, we really have to pay attention to that. Did God really say it this way, or it come from the theologians who have the blood of Adam in them? Hosea 4:6, "My people are destroyed for lack of knowledge, because you have rejected knowledge, I also will reject you from being a servant to Me; because you have forgotten the Law of God, and follow what men say instead of what I say; I also will forget you, My child" (Paraphrase). Today we believe more the words of men than in the Words of God, and it is totally unscriptural. This is why the devil wants you to have doubts, to speak his words, and to speak it negatively. It will destroy you and tear you down over time. Faith comes by hearing, and hearing, and hearing, and hearing, the Word of God. Now listen to this. Faith in the devil word will work as well for you when you say it, and say it, and say it, and say it outch. Faith is believing what you are saying. When you speak, doubts "IF" is the biggest problem in all doubt's words, and it is so hard to see also. God will never ever speak like that; except He does now in the Bible. God wants you to be Healthy, He wants you to have Abundance, to live longer, to have Faith like Him. Did you know that you can have abundance speaking the words of the devil also? (That you will never hear this in your church) When you have fear of this, fear of that, fear of travel, and the devil said: I can arrange that for you to receive. I have doubts of this and of that. I don't know will I have that job, I doubt that, I can arrange that for you to receive, say the devil. I'm poor, I have no money, I can't join both ends, I can't afford that, I can arrange that for you to receive what you say. I'm sick, I think that I am getting the cold, cancer is something that I am very afraid of, I can arrange that for you to receive say the devil, as long that it is according to your mouth. This is the choice we make, and we cannot blame anyone, except ourselves. As a born-again person, you should be aware of all that, because when you will try to enter Heaven with all that baggage in your heart, and you might hear Jesus say: "I do not know you, depart from Me," outch. The Bible is loaded of doubts words, "IF is the biggest of all, "BUT" is a semi/doubt, not as powerful, only, there is plainly in the Bible. We have to thank these men of religion; they really succeeded in putting the words of their father in it. The more damages are in the "New Covenant," they put them in the mouth of God, Matthew, Mark, Luke, John, Paul, Timothy, Titus, James, Peter, Philemon, Jude, Jesus, and the mouth of the Holy Spirit. Faith is something that is very powerful from both sides of the fence. Personally, I love Thanksgiving prayers, because I already receive by my own words that I really believe in them. One of the things I do when I say a Thanksgiving prayer is to thank God for what I did ask. Let's say that I pray about that new job that I will believe I have (By Faith). I will say thank You for that new job, Father, say it many times a day. Also, I said to myself to help me to receive faster. Faith comes by hearing, and hearing the word of Normand. I say it a few times with a smile and I am very glad, and I laugh also, clap my hands, because I did receive---by Faith. You can do the way you want it, and I don't think that anyone ever teaches about, to how to receive faster? It works for me, and I do enjoy it. Sometimes you do what you have to do. Ephesians 2:10, For we are his workmanship, created in Christ Jesus for good works, which God prepared beforehand that we should walk in them. Matthew 15:11, Not what goes into the mouth that defiles a man/woman. There is one thing that the devil does not want you to read is the fact that you are a new creature in Christ Jesus. The fact is that you are His workmanship (God) and not your own. Matthew 15:13-14, Jesus said," Every plant (We are a seed that God did has planted) which My Father has not planted will be uprooted. Let them alone, they are blind leaders of the blind. When the blind lead the blind, both will fall into a ditch. There is no blind in Heaven, and there is no ditch either. So, all of you preachers who are the leaders of your congregation, you are better to start to pay attention at what's coming out of your mouth, from now on, people will start to pay attention, and God too." You will not even know it that you are speaking doubt Ly when you quote the Bible, and there is an "IF" and "BUT" in these quotes. Be aware because your words will judge you at the end. When you will be dismissing my teaching, you will be more blind than you thought, and you will be preaching in blindness. It is not an easy thing to do, to stop using "IF" or "BUT" in your language of every day. We have spoken that language since we were 3 years old, and we hear these two words so often in a day, it is not an easy thing to do. Don't forget, laziness is very much alive, so to speak. It will demand a lot for each individual to start changing to way they speak. Do it by Faith and believe that it will be easy. I speak two languages, and I have to re-train myself to not use these two doubtful words, and God wants us to speak just like Him.

"When it's not right don't do it;

when it's not true don't say it"

(Marcus Aurelius) (121-180 AD)

Romans 8:16-17, The Spirit Himself bears witness with our spirit that we are Children of God, and when Children, then Heirs---Heirs of God and joint Heirs with Christ, when indeed we suffer with Him, that we may be also Glorified together. God says that you can have what you are saying. When you say, I think I'm getting a cold, or I am sick. I know that you are thinking that it is ok to say; I am sick, because I am telling the truth, I am sick. Do not say it, that's what I am saying, even when you are sick, (Now that you are sick –and the next time that sickness arrive think ahead and speak the answer, and you will see a big difference) it's not because the package is in your body that you can have it, and keep it. Thank the Lord God, because you did give it to Him, thank Jesus because it is by His stripes that we are healed, thank God because you already did receive it by Faith. It's not because you are sick, depressed, sad, poor, no job, etc. that you have to say the problem out loud. Say the answer instead, and believe that answer is already yours---by Faith. Do you do just talk, and not really pay attention to your words, did you know that you we were talking about the problem? I will say no, you did not pay attention, because it is a habit, we have to act the same way as we always act, only by habits, and it will hurt you later. We should confess often to not let no words of our enemy or corrupt communication come out of our mouth. That will be good for me and the hearer also, so that we can both be edified. Your Faith words will make you a winner when you are speaking Faithfully. Fear words will destroy you, over and over, same as your "sick" words will make you sick over and over. This is why we have to really pay attention at what we are saying at all times. Don't forget about the Law in Genesis, is that everything produces after its kind. That you speak poverty, fear, sickness, you will produce it, ---- after their own kind. God did create man and woman to his own image, spirit, soul, and body, until we will return to Him. Our spirit only, not the body, it will return to dust. God wants us to imitate Him. When you speak Satan's words, you are actually imitating him, and you don't even know that. Outch and outch again. 1 John 5:4, For whatever is born of God overcomes the world. This is the Victory that has overcome the world ---- our Faith (In His Word). So, say it a few times a day, take some notes for yourself. I am a world overcomer because I am born of God. Don't say it in your head; you have a mouth, then use it. Faith comes by hearing, and hearing the words of .... (Put your name) Confess Victory when you are facing defeat.

Confess healing when your body feels sick. Confess abundance when looking at your situation that you are in. This is a quote from Charles Capps: God was speaking to Charles. I HAVE TOLD MY PEOPLE THEY CAN HAVE WHAT THEY SAY, AND THEY ARE SAYING WHAT THEY HAVE. 2 Corinthians 4:18, We do not look at the things which are seen, only at the things which are not seen. For the things which are seen are temporary, and the things which are not seen are Eternal. Satan's goal is to destroy the earth, piece by piece, with storm, flood, volcano, tsunami, and now he is concentring to destroy the Word of God in the mind and hearts of us the God's people, and putting in his own words, so, that we can continue to believe that we are sick, poor, and unworthy. The devil he is already defeated, 1992 years ago. Try to remind him or his demons about the cross, and you will see that he will come out of your mind fast. The unbelievers confess with their mouth daily; it is like a Thanksgiving prayer without prayer. They confess prosperity, they talk prosperity, they are unbelievers per - se, and they make video of 3 to 10 seconds long in their mind to help themselves to believe what they saw with their eyes of Faith, and this is why they receive. They do not exactly know how it works, only that it works. They continue to say daily what they want, and they will have them, according to their heart. So, the unbelievers are sowing, and sowing, and they receive a big harvest. They sow and they reap. It is only temporal though. Be careful to not falling in love with material things. You can have it only; do not fall in love with it. The treasure of your heart depends of what you did put in, in the first place. The devil did programme our minds to speak his words so that we do not need to resist him. He did find a clever way to do it, and people into this entire world speak his language every day, and they are not even aware of it. John 12:47-50, Jesus is saying:" When anyone hears My Words and does not believe, I do not judge him/her; for I did not come to judge the world, only to save the world. He/she who rejects Me, and does not receive My Words, has that which judges him/her --the Word that I have spoken will judge him/her in the last day. For I have not spoken of My own Authority; and the Father Who sent Me gives Me a command what I should say, and what I should speak. I know that His command is Everlasting Life, therefore, whatever I speak, just as the Father has told Me, so I speak." God never prays the problem, He is always praying the solution, and He spoke the desired results, and we should do the same. Faith come by hearing and hearing, and hearing the word of................
(Put your name)

"The truth can walk around Naked;

the lie has to be clothed"

(Yiddish proverb)

What I am ready to tell you will not be easy to understand, and will demand that everyone put really aside everything you already know about that subject, (Male spirit) and pay attention to what I am describing, it is the real Truth. Of course, it has to be according to the Word of God, and not according to the words of men in the Bible, or mine. I can back up what I will be saying to you. You will have to put a lot of effort and understanding from your part, before you will start to believe it. Most likely not at first, so, I want you to check it out, and open your mind, and listen carefully at all this information that I will throw at you, because I am touching a very serious subject, so, here it is.

A male spirit will produce another male spirit. Well, that information wasn't much, will you say, wait, there is more. When I say that a male spirit will produce another male spirit, I am not talking about a man's sperm producing another male. A man's sperm can produce a male and female human being when he gives his donation to a female human being. They will have to work together to be able to produce another human being. I understand all that. The subject here is a "Male spirit," not a human being. A man and a woman can produce another human being, except they cannot create a spirit per - se. They will produce a human being who will come with a spirit, except that they cannot create that spirit in that human being. It is the man with his seed that will produce that human being. It is God who put that seed (Spirit), in the woman's egg; it is not the sperm of man. The woman is the receiver of that new human being; the man needs a partner working with him to achieve that goal. He cannot do it on his own; he needs someone who can do it with him. So, they can produce another human, only they cannot create that being, who is **a male spirit** in a male or female body. when you will see in the text the words, They, Us, Our, Them, We, it will be to describe the Holy Spirit, the Words, and God, all together at once. Eve came from Adam; They didn't use Adam's sperm to create the spirit of Eve; They did use a being (Spirit) to produce another being (Spirit) who already existed, and that being is Adam. Same way with an oak tree, you can produce another oak that already exist; they yield seed. Genesis 1:11, Whose seed is in itself. (After its own kind) God said that the herb, the grass, and the animals, according to its kind to multiply on the earth. God said: Let **us** make man in Our image, according to Our likeness. Adam is a male spirit, and God said that (Everything) will produce after its own kind, except God said to us He said according to Our likeness. We know for a fact that Eve had a female body, and that she came from Adam, well, that's not really true that she came from Adam, she came from the spirit of Adam. Bear with me because it's becoming interesting, I know I told you it will not be easy to comprehend. When we pay attention to the detail, we know that Adam had a male spirit and was a male human being. Therefore, when Eve was created by **Them**, she had to be reproduced the same thing Adam was---a male spirit, and happen to have a female human body. Can you see it now that **They** did reproduce a new male spirit, that came from another male spirit, who already existed. (Adam) (After its kind) In Genesis 2:21, It said that **They** did use a "rib" from Adam, and in verse 22, **They** (not He) made into a woman. (From the rib) I am telling you it is not the truth, it is a lie, not coming from God, or from the Holy Spirit, only the ones who have "Dirty fingers", the theologians and scholars, they are the only ones who can have said these lies. God did not write the Bible it was the theologians and scholars who wrote It. It is impossible for **Them** to use a **human being's rib** to make another human being, with a spirit in it that comes from that rib. It's impossible. God said in Genesis 1:26, Let **us** make man in Our image, according to Our likeness. God was not alone in all this, He said; Let **us**, also, to **Our likeness**, and **They** are all male Spirits. So, **They**, created a male spirit with a human body, who has a male spirit. (Eve) So, afterward Genesis 2:18, God said: "It is not good that man should be alone; I will make him a helper **comparable to him**. Comparable also means "**like**" (Exactly the same) Genesis 2:21, "God caused a "Deep" sleep to fall from Adam. I do believe that **They** operated in Adam's spirit so that **They** will be able to bring another new male spirit; **it has to be comparable**, a male spirit producing another male spirit. So, now you understand that They had to use a male spirit to be able to have another male spirit (After Our likeness) (Not a rib) When it's said that **They** use a rib to create another human being, we know that Adam had a penis, and that **They** will reproduce another human with another spirit to come from Adam's spirit. **They** will have to create another human being **comparable with a penis also.** Because They did use a rib, according to the theologians and scholars. We (male/female) are the "Likeness" of God, Holy Spirit, and the Word, and **They** are all male Spirit, so, **They,** are not a rib, they are **Spirits.** Because, when **They** did create the first male spirit (**Like They are**), who is Adam, who was created just as **Our likeness a** male spirit. We created a male spirit like **Our likeness, because God, the Word, and the Holy Spirit are** male Spirits, who will be in a human male body, who happens to have a penis. Them **They** do not have one "a penis". **They** did not create a woman. They created a new male spirit, with a human body, with a different gender, that we call a woman. We can see that these idiot theologians and bad scholars try to make it a beautiful story for us to believe, except, it doesn't make sense that the Holy Spirit misspoke when telling all this to Moses. The first page in the Bible and already a lot of controversy, because of people who happen to have a "**lack of knowledge**" in all this. It is impossible for God to lie, and He didn't take the whole credit for Himself; this is why He said;' Let **us** make man in Our image, according to Our likeness. (That's why They didn't use a rib, They, use a spirit who was already in existence to create another spirit who the gender was a female. Adam was a spirit and They created after its own kind) These theologians and scholars did not give credit to anyone else, except God, so you can see that they do not pay attention to the very detail in everything they read. (God did say Our likeness, not My likeness) Only Normand paid attention and will continue to do so. Now the question is: "Who will you believe"?

Theologians and scholars, or a ninth-grade education man.

The end.